PICK UP THE DAMN PHONE!

HOW PEOPLE, NOT TECHNOLOGY, SEAL THE DEAL

JOANNE S. BLACK

Booktrope Editions
Seattle WA 2013

Cover Design by Jennifer Rogers Tyson

Edited by Taylor Mallory Holland

PRINT ISBN 978-1-935961-46-8

EPUB ISBN 978-1-62015-050-4

Library of Congress Control Number: 2013917525

This book is dedicated to the next generation—my grandchildren. To Max, Melody, Ella, and Nate, I hope that you will always enjoy talking to people, that you will love conversation, and that you'll know when to put away your toys and connect with the world around you. Always remember the wonderful times we've shared and how much I love you.

In Memoriam—My Parents

Eunice Green Schlesinger

Nathan Samuel Schlesinger

Who never lived to share the joys of my life

ACKNOWLEDGMENTS

None of us would be where we are or who we are without our family and dear friends. In that vein, I'd like to thank:

My husband, Bruce—who loves me no matter what I look like or what I do, and who continues to tell me how proud he is of me.

My sister, Jill—who is my dearest friend, my confidante, and the best travel buddy ... ever.

My daughter, Judy—who lights up every room she enters. She is my friend, my inspiration, and my final editor.

My daughter, Dana—whom I can call anytime for advice, and whose passion for following her dreams is unwavering.

My sons-in-law, Adam and Brent—two of the best guys in the world, who celebrate my accomplishments as if I was their own mother.

Aunt Leona and Uncle Joel—who were my second parents, and who always delighted in my family and my achievements.

Aunt Ruthie and Uncle David, Aunt Marilyn and Uncle Milton, Aunt Gert and Uncle Marty—whose love for each other and our family continues to inspire me.

My dear friend, Susan—my own private cheerleader, whose friendship and encouragement are unparalleled.

I'd also like to express my sincere gratitude for the special people who helped me bring this book to life:

Taylor Mallory Holland—who is the best editor a writer could have. I think she knows my content and my voice better than I do.

The No More Cold Calling team (including Christy Whelan, Kelsey Jones, John Muldoon, David Kerr, Aidan Crawford, and Judy Lewenthal Daniel)—who keep my referral passion alive with their diligence and enthusiasm.

Jennifer Rogers Tyson of LeftRight Collaborative—who designed a "wow" cover for this book.

The team at Booktrope Publishing—who immediately loved *Pick Up the Damn Phone!* and gathered a great group of talented people to ensure my book was the best it could be.

CONTENTS

INTRODUCTION

YOU ARE THE ULTIMATE SALES TECHNOLOGY

It's Not 140 Characters; It's You ...

This was the title of a blog post I wrote several years ago about how to attract sales prospects in a technology-focused world. Since then, social media has continued to grow in popularity, usage, and complexity, but my point—that people, not tweets, seal the deal—is just as true today.

Whether you read this book in 2013, 2023, or 3013, you will witness much change throughout your lifetime. But one thing never changes: People do business with people, not with technology.

At least I hope that doesn't change. Maybe I'm wrong, and a day will come when people stop talking to each other and instead communicate solely through technology. I won't be around then, but I want my grandchildren, great-grandchildren, and great-great-grandchildren to know what it's like to be human—to use words, to make connections, to enjoy seeing someone smile, and to smile back.

The digital world—as great as it is—threatens personal connections. Humans need face-to-face contact with others. Even with whisper-light computing power and immediate, 140-character Twitter posts, we are a face-to-face species, one that thrives on interpersonal communication and being in the presence of like-minded individuals working together for a common goal. Email, texting, social networking—these certainly have a place in business today, but none of them replaces the power of an in-person connection.

Old Doesn't Necessarily Mean Irrelevant

You've heard it: Television will kill radio. Video killed the radio star. And social media and the Internet will eliminate the time-consuming, face-to-face aspect of sales. Um, no.

I am not, I assure you, a technology neophyte or a Luddite. Like many of you, I happily, eagerly, and creatively embrace the new solutions that technology and the Web provide—when it makes sense to do so. Marketing automation, CRM, social media, and other technological tools enable us to sell more efficiently and cost effectively. But the most powerful tool in your sales toolbox is still you!

What's the best way to reach, communicate with, develop, and sell to your key audience? If you think back over your most successful business deals, I bet face-to-face, person-to-person, high-touch communication—a phone call, a video conference, or (best of all) an in-person meeting—has accelerated your sales process time and time again.

If you want that extra edge, then come out from behind the cloak of technology. The personal connection seals the deal every time!

> If you want that extra edge, then come out from behind the cloak of technology. The personal connection seals the deal every time!

Now, About This Book

After years of colleagues asking if I had written a book, I decided it was time to write about my passion—referral selling. In April 2006, Warner Business Books published *No More Cold Calling*™. Soon after, people started asking when I would write my next book, and I vehemently answered, "Never. *No More Cold Calling* is my legacy."

I still believe my first book is my legacy. Every word in it is just as true today as it was then. Yet, there have been fundamental shifts in the business world in the intervening years. So I'm back—with new perspectives and content about what these changes mean for salespeople.

The biggest changes in the sales world have been the rapid growth of social media, the emergence of the cloud, increased mobility, and a myriad of innovative technologies. Do I use technology? Yes. Do I write about it? Yes. Do I have a point of view about it? Yes. But technology is not my passion, so this is not a how-to book about using technology to sell.

Instead, this book focuses on the intersection of sales, technology, and referrals—the marriage of the old (relationships) with the new (technology). Each of these has its place in sales. In fact, they are interwoven, interdependent, and inextricably connected. We will explore these connections and discuss how to leverage the invaluable sales intelligence that technology provides—and how to know when it's time to put away the toys and have a grown-up, face-to-face conversation.

We'll examine how technology has *and hasn't* changed the sales landscape. It's certainly changed the way we gather information about prospects. It's also changed how they gather information about us and what they expect of us. And let's face it, if you're not active on social media, you're about five steps behind. But when it comes to *how* we sell (you know, one person to another) not much has changed.

I interviewed dozens of sales and marketing executives for this book, asking for their points of view on selling in the digital world—how they use technology, what is and isn't working, and which traps to avoid. I also asked what they wished their sales-people would do more of, less of, or differently. As you might expect, whenever we ask sales professionals for opinions, we get a variety of perspectives. I'll share these differences with you and let you know if I agree ... or not.

Referral selling is not a "nice to have," but a "must have," sales initiative.

My point of view (and I was surprised that most of these experts agree) remains that referral selling is the most productive, effective, and efficient prospecting strategy. In fact, I'm now even *more convinced* that salespeople leave money on the table every day, because they don't adopt a disciplined referral-selling strategy. Referral selling is not a "nice to have," but a "must have," sales initiative.

Many people consider my views contrarian and—in the established school of traditional sales—heretical thinking. I ask you to keep an open mind, just as I did when interviewing these thought leaders. The sales landscape changes hourly. If we follow the same path everyone else follows, we won't stand out, and we'll lose our competitive edge. Have the guts to carve your own path—whether you're the CEO of a global corporation, an entrepreneur, head of a sales team, or a seasoned salesperson.

Best Regards,

Joanne

Joanne S. Black

September, 2013

SECTION 1

SALES 2.0: EVERYTHING (AND NOTHING) HAS CHANGED

The New Normal. Sales 2.0. Sales 3.0—heck, there might even be Sales 6.0 by the time you read this.

There's always someone who wants to be famous for inventing a new moniker. But there's no such thing as a "New Normal." In fact, there's no such thing as "normal," because as the old saying goes, change is life's only constant.

Business moves at such a fast pace that the challenge is to stay ahead of the curve. What can you do that's different from the next guy? What sets you apart? What have you thought of, developed, and/or implemented that's never been done before? What's so exciting about what you're doing that people line up to get on your train?

In the sales world, pundits were quick to compare the old way of selling (Sales 1.0) with the new way (Sales 2.0). In short, the comparison looks like this:

- Sales 1.0 was about rigidly following processes, while Sales 2.0 is about helping prospects buy.
- Sales 1.0 meant counting every activity, while Sales 2.0 focuses on measuring activities that count.
- Sales 1.0 was volume versus relationships, while Sales 2.0 is about relationship-driven value.
- Sales 1.0 meant mass prospecting, while Sales 2.0 provides a network of unlimited opportunities.
- Sales 1.0 was about selling solutions, while Sales 2.0 is about helping customers succeed.

Experts were also quick to tell us that technology changes everything—that Sales 2.0 is an entirely new way of working. And I was one of the first to scream: "No, no, no!" Good salespeople have always listened; helped their prospects make the correct buying decisions; built strong, lasting relationships; and maintained and nurtured networks of colleagues, clients, and prospects.

The Internet is the most powerful, life- and business-changing tool created in generations. For example, when was the last time you looked up a telephone number in an otherwise-used-as-a-booster-seat phone book? But is it the end-all, be-all for our business challenges and sales solutions? I don't think so.

> Our smartest, tried-and-true business-development, lead-generation, deal-closing tool is and has always been ourselves. And that's not going to change anytime soon—if ever.

Bottom line: Sales is still about people selling to people. Our smartest, tried-and-true business-development, lead-generation, deal-closing tool is and has always been ourselves. And that's not going to change anytime soon—if ever.

What *has* changed is the access buyers and sellers have to *information.* Barry Trailer, managing partner and co-founder of CSO Insights,[1] provides a compelling description of Sales 2.0:

> Sales 2.0 focuses on aligning steps in the sales cycle with those in the buying cycle by leveraging technology, process improvement, and sales knowledge to effectively collaborate with the most appropriate individuals (internally and externally) and doing so in the preferred format of each.
>
> Sales 2.0 does not necessarily change *what* salespeople do; it changes *how* they work to become more efficient and effective.
>
> 2.0 sales reps are able to collaborate with participants on both sides of the buy-sell equation. For many, this is not a radical departure from but rather an extension of the relationships and conversations they have always sought to facilitate. The mindset being that a knowledgeable buyer is in the end not only a better buyer but a more satisfied customer.

Call it Sales 2.0 or 3.0, or whatever you want to call it. At the end of the day, our jobs remain the same. Great salespeople have always asked good questions, discovered their clients' needs, and offered solutions. Why is this now new? Because someone felt compelled to create a graph and make a comparison?

---

[1] Barry Trailer, "What is Sales 2.0?", *customerTHINK*, http://www.customerthink.com/article/what_is_sales_2_0 (June 4, 2009).

Executives are busy people. Most don't have "meet with salesperson" at the top of their to-do lists. Our job as smart, strategic sales pros is to deliver value—real value. And technology won't do that for us, nor will it give us a huge advantage over our competitors, who (let's face it) have access to the same gadgets, gizmos, and applications.

What seals the deal today is the same thing that sealed the deal back in the days of the three-martini lunch—having a personal connection to prospects, understanding what our buyers want from us, and delivering results.

However, some things *have changed*—including what buyers want and expect from us, why expertise is important, and how technology can help us better manage and leverage our most powerful connections.

Buyer 2.0

Welcome to the age of the informed consumer, or the digital buyer … or "Buyer 2.0."

Once upon a time, in the days before Google, Amazon, Yelp, and social media, clients looked to salespeople for information about our companies, products, and services. Often, we were their only resource for such knowledge.

Now with a few clicks of a mouse, they can learn all about us—including what people are saying about our companies, how our products and solutions work, and what our competitors have to offer.

This is a significant shift in professional selling. After all, when was the last time you needed (or *wanted*) a salesperson to walk you through all of the details about a product?

Buyer 2.0 is very good at homework. In fact, 86 percent of business buyers engage in research independent of the sales cycle, according to a 2011 study from Forrester.[2] Before they make

[2] Forrester Research, Inc., "Q1 2011 US and European B2B Social Technographics® Online Survey For Business Technology," http://www.forrester.com/2011+Social+Technographics174+For+Business+Technology+Buyers/fulltext/-/E-RES58564 (Oct. 11, 2011).

contact with us, our buyers have usually checked us out, compared pricing, read a white paper or two, listened to a webinar, and/or viewed a demo. They've also researched our competition.

Then comes what Jim Blasingame, author of *The Age of the Customer* series, calls the "moment of relevance"—the point at which customers have completed their research and are ready to make a decision. This is when they rule us in or out, which means we want to be there—top of mind and first in line—when this moment comes along.

Sure, our buyers can learn most of what they need to know about our products online, and if we're smart, we'll make it easy for them to access relevant information. But salespeople still have a role to play during the information-gathering portion of the buying cycle. We must stay in touch with our buyers, share examples of clients with similar challenges, and learn about their budgets, decision-making criteria, and buying processes. Above all, we must craft a compelling return on investment (ROI) scenario, so that the decision to buy is no longer a choice, but a given.

Sure, our buyers can learn most of what they need to know about our products online, and if we're smart, we'll make it easy for them to access relevant information. But salespeople still have a role to play during the information-gathering portion of the buying cycle.

David Nour, author of *Relationship Economics,* says we should use social analytics to identify the digital buyer. Then we can build and nurture digital relationships with these buyers, customize the experience, allow for interaction, and customize the next interaction based on what we learned from this one. "Forget CRM," he says. "It's 'DRM'—digital relationship management—and we are catering to what they need, when they need it, on the device of their choice."

This is great advice for those selling a very simple product or solution en masse. In this case, you can usually satisfy your buyers' need for information and guidance with automation—by offering a variety of choices online, or providing Web chats and questionnaires so they feel confident about their decisions.

However, for those of us who sell services or more complex business solutions, our buyers need more from us. They need real, live, experienced salespeople to help them wade through all the options and information and find the right product or solution for their businesses. They need choices and direction.

Steve Woods, former chief technology officer for Eloqua and now group vice president of software development at Oracle, says today's sales rep is an "information concierge." He explains that in the pre-Internet era, back when information was a rare commodity, salespeople were the gatekeepers of information. But now that anyone can access content on just about any topic, the role of salespeople is to help clients and prospects get the information they want and need, when they want and need it. "Companies that understand this shift build 'content assets' for their salespeople," Steve says. "These assets are not salesy. They don't promote the company but instead offer fun, interesting, and unique stories and ideas, so that salespeople can use relevant content to build relationships."

This means that we, as salespeople, must get to know our clients—not just their demographics and how they spend money online, but what they actually want and need from *us*.

YOUR BUYER DOESN'T KNOW IT ALL

It's been said that today's consumers are so informed they have usually decided whether to buy before they ever speak to a salesperson. In fact, research from SiriusDecisions shows that 67 percent of the buyer's journey is now done digitally. Some take this to mean that our prospects and clients don't really need us anymore—that the automation of selling has made salespeople irrelevant. Not true!

As Megan Heuer, vice president of data-driven marketing at SiriusDecisions, writes in her blog, "Three Myths of the '67 Percent' Statistic":[3]

> Just because buyers spend time online doesn't mean sales is not involved at all stages of the buyer's journey, including the early and late stages. It is true that the standard is now higher for sales to add value to the conversation, because so much information can be found online.

---

[3]Megan Heuer, "Three Myths of the '67 Percent' Statistic," *SiriusDecisions*, http://www.siriusdecisions.com/blog/three-myths-of-the-67-percent-statistic/ (July 3, 2013).

> Information isn't knowledge. Knowledge comes with wisdom, experience, and a clear vision of the big picture

There's no denying that today's buyers are armed with plenty of information, and this has certainly changed the dynamic of our client relationships. But information isn't knowledge. Knowledge comes with wisdom, experience, and a clear vision of the big picture—not just the immediate problem at hand, which is often all our clients, without the benefit of our experience, can see. They know they need "something," but do they really know what that is? Not always. In fact, not usually. That's why they need us.

It's our job to ensure customers get the correct solutions for their business challenges. Great salespeople know how to uncover the core issues plaguing clients so we can make the best possible recommendations. We're not "yes men." Clients want our points of view. They want to learn best practices, and they want to hear what doesn't work.

The Customer Is NOT Always Right

Jim Mallory, director of marketing for e2b teknologies, says he often encounters prospects who think they have identified the right software for their business challenges. However, once Jim's salespeople ask questions—the smart, information-gathering, critical questions that uncover their prospects' real problems—the solutions are often far removed from the buyers' original concerns.

For example, when Jim's company received an email from a new prospect who knew about their impressive track record and was prepared to close a six-figure deal in less than a month, Jim and his associates were shocked. No one had even met with the buyer, and their sales cycle with most new clients lasted six months to a year. But after Jim's team met with the buyer and learned about his needs, they realized this client would fare better with an entirely different product.

They could have rushed the deal and pocketed the easy money. Instead, they put the brakes on the done-deal and took time to show the client a better solution—proving themselves trustworthy experts and impressing a new client (and future referral source).

Tell Them Where It Hurts

When prospects come to us, they have problems that need to be solved—pain that needs addressing. And while they know it hurts, they're often unclear about exactly where the pain is coming from and how to fix it. That's where salespeople come in. We know our industries; we know our products; and most importantly, we know our clients. So with a little investigating, we can show them exactly where it hurts.

This is particularly true when you're meeting with high-level decision-makers—who want assurance (as quickly as possible) that you know exactly how to alleviate their pain. A study of 125 senior-level executives by Responsibility Centered Leadership found that most executives only give salespeople five minutes on the initial call to develop some sort of beneficial relationship.[4]

---

[4] Kent J. Gregoire, "Selling at the Executive Level: A summary of studies examining how client executives view their relationships with professional salespeople," Responsibility Centered Leadership, 2011.

During those five minutes, they want reps to:

- Speak from a business perspective, demonstrating they've done their homework and developed an understanding of the executive's key business issues.
- Introduce relevant questions and share new business perspectives.
- Listen and understand, rather than attempt to sell something during the first meeting.

Today's buyers are overloaded with information, options, and research. That's why they need us—their "information concierges"—to connect the dots between their business challenges and our solutions.

WHO'S IN CONTROL?

Technology—and all of the information it provides—has made buyers a little ... well, cocky. They know what they want (or at least, think they do), and they want it now. If they are not having a stellar experience with your company, they will simply double-click on the next name on the list.

While I'm all for empowering customers, Buyer 2.0 isn't the only one armed with new information-gathering technology. Seller 2.0 has access to all sorts of tech tools that enable us to learn more about our customers—their demographics, interests, needs, and wants. And given our experience, we know exactly how to deliver the value they want in a timely manner and at a price point they can live with.

Technology expedites many tasks, but at the end of the day, clients need us.

Technology expedites many tasks, but at the end of the day, clients need us. When you travel by air, you no longer need a person to provide the schedule, sell you a ticket, or issue your boarding pass. But you want a person to greet you on the plane and to ensure there's a pilot in the cockpit. The same applies when you purchase a car. You can configure it online, but you still want a service person there to answer your questions and to treat you well.

Bottom line: While our customers might want to drive the car, they still need us to steer.

Should You Let the Client Drive?

David Satterwhite, vice president of worldwide sales at Appcelerator and former vice president of America sales for Good Technology, says we now focus far more on the buying cycle than ever before. "Customers are much less willing to let salespeople lead formal sales cycles," he says. "They want to define the terms of the 'partnership.'"

When David negotiates large-enterprise deals, he levels the playing field by saying to the customer: "It's not my job to dictate how you want to buy. You let us know." David says some customers buy in small chunks over time while others want to leverage a volume purchase and bring down the price. "This approach lowers everyone's anxiety level," he says. "We're no longer a vendor, but a partner."

Keep Your Hands on the Steering Wheel

Here's where it gets tricky. Our clients expect to have more control over the buying cycle. But at the same time, they want the lowest possible price. And these two desires can be mutually-exclusive.

Geoff Ashley, former director of business development at SAP Americas and principal of PROe, says many companies have an "I sell the way you buy" mentality. In other words, salespeople keep saying yes.

For example, if you sell software, and the prospects ask if the screen can be blue, you say yes. If they want a field moved or created, you say yes. Even if they want entirely new functionality created, you say yes. They can have all these things … for a price. After all, it takes time and resources to customize your product for every client.

For instance, many software companies and other similar vendors have moved away from on-premise software with licensing rights to a cloud-computing model, which is less complex and usually cheaper. But saying yes to everything the customer wants negates the purpose of this transition. That's why we must help our clients understand that they need to buy the way we sell, and that doing so cuts their costs.

This is where a great salesperson can really make a difference. Our clients may already know what we do and how we do it. But that doesn't mean they know exactly what they need from us, and how to get it most efficiently and cost effectively. They don't know the traps to avoid and what doesn't work. They usually don't fully understand the commitment needed (from themselves and their teams) to implement solutions that guarantee knock-your-socks-off ROI. But *we* do.

So go ahead and let your client drive the car. Just make sure you're there to navigate.

Buyer 2.0 Wants It All—Right Now

Technology may make us faster, better, stronger, etc. But it has also made us much less patient.

Buyer 2.0 expects us to move quickly, to deliver solutions and results almost immediately. To some degree, technology enables us to do that. But a word of warning: Faster does not always mean better. Speed often makes us careless, sloppy, less thorough, and more likely to make mistakes.

Brian Schlosser, vice president of global accounts for the Information Intelligence Group at EMC, has an interesting perspective on this issue. He says:

> Today it is easier to connect with customers and co-workers. Twenty-five years ago, I sent a letter and waited at least a week for a response. A fax cut it down to a few hours. A phone call had to be during business hours, and often you had to wait for your prospect's secretary to give him the message. Now emails arrive in seconds. But I still text colleagues, because email is too slow. My phone even lets certain people ring through to me in the middle of the night.

Sound familiar? The problem, he says, is that all of these changes are about acceleration and removing friction in the sales cycle. If you do things right, you succeed more quickly. But if you make mistakes, you have no time to recover. "While our customers demand speed, they are no more tolerant of errors than before," Brian says. "Going fast badly doesn't make you successful. Yet, we are at great risk of emphasizing speed and ignoring quality."

Be Realistic

There's an old saying in sales: Good, fast, cheap. Pick two.

If you want top quality and want it fast, be prepared to pay a premium. *Cheap* and *quality* don't belong in the same sentence. You get what you pay for. Clients who try to beat you down on price will continue to expect the same level of expertise and responsiveness. If you're a low-cost provider, then you probably have a fulfillment process that is automated and efficient. If, however, you sell a more complex product or service, forget fast and cheap.

There's an old saying in sales: Good, fast, cheap. Pick two.

So how do you work more quickly without sacrificing quality? Andy Paul, author of *Zero-Time Selling,* says the answer is to have a repeatable process with accountability and metrics. However, most companies get new customers and then quickly move on to the next prospect. They ignore current clients—who are their best source of new business. It's like recreating the wheel. The goal is to fine-tune a sales process that enables us to stay in touch with customers, assess metrics, and gather results, while also working faster and more efficiently.

> If I provide a referral and you don't follow up, why would I ever refer you again?

Be Prepared

Clients value speed, which means we must always be prepared to move quickly when opportunities arise. A 2011 survey from InsideSales.com shows that, for inquiries submitted on the Web, 78 percent of deals went to the first companies that responded.[5] Yet, 35 to 63 percent of companies failed to respond at all.[6] Amazing! Speed counts, and we drop the ball when we don't follow up quickly.

I'm always baffled when salespeople tell me they have referral opportunities sitting on their desks or in their inboxes that they haven't acted on. Are we understaffed, overwhelmed, or just lazy? When people refer you, follow up immediately. That means in the next hour, not the next day, week, or month. Failure to do so is an affront to your referral source. You appear arrogant, self-centered, and careless.

If I provide a referral and you don't follow up, why would I ever refer you again? It would be obvious you don't value our relationship, and you certainly wouldn't value the connection I offered. Your lack of responsiveness and enthusiasm would send a clear message that you don't care. And if you don't care about me, I don't care about you. We're done.

---

[5] Raghu Raghavan and David Elkington, "Increase Lead Cycle Velocity and Close More Deals," InsideSales.com, 2011.
[6] David Elkington, "B2B Lead Roundtable: Research from Harvard, MIT Pinpoints Hard Lead Conversion Lessons with Easy Solutions," InsideSales.com.

Be Thorough

In *Zero-Time Selling*, Andy Paul writes:

> For any business, the speed of selling is inextricably linked to responsiveness [which] is composed of two elements: Content and speed. A quick but incomplete response to a customer's question is the same as no response at all. A complete but slow response ... is marginally better than no response. Given the trove of information available on the Internet about every type of product and service, if a buyer still has a question for a seller after doing online research, then their need for an answer is, by definition, urgent and critical.

Andy highlights an important sales challenge: The need to respond quickly *and* thoroughly.

A study by DemandGen and Genius.com[7] found that 95 percent of B2B customers chose the vendors that provided ample information to navigate each step of their buying processes. In other words, if you can't make it quick and easy to do business with you, they'll find someone who can.

Be Accurate

When it comes to information, quality is just as important as quantity. Sloppiness is a huge turnoff for savvy buyers. I've worked with vendors who are in such a hurry to respond that their

---

[7] Matt West and Andrew Gaffney, "Inside the Mind of the B2B Buyer: Influences Outside the Funnel," DemandGen Report and Genius.com, 2010.

grammar and punctuation are terrible, their URLs don't work, and they've only answered one of my two questions. Why would I work with people who are so careless? They'd probably drop the ball on my project and miss deadlines. I would have no confidence that I was a priority.

Yes, I would come to that conclusion simply from reading a poorly-written or incomplete email. When you're communicating with prospects—in person, on the Web, or on the phone—you must show up professionally ... every single time.

I repeat: Good, fast, cheap. Pick two.

Clients Buy You!

When it comes to B2B sales, clients are not just buying your product or service; they're paying for your expertise. They are accountable for results, and their jobs are on the line. They want to do business with people who know their stuff, who know how to deliver results, and who offer something a little different, better, or more targeted than competitors. Be specific, relevant, and concise, and clients will seek you out. The age of the generalist is gone.

Ian Brodie, a marketing coach based in the U.K., agrees. "If a client comes to you with the notion you are the leader, you're ahead of the game," he says. "Clients get surface knowledge for free on the Web. They don't get wisdom and the practical experience of people who have done the work."

There are at least three benefits of expertise: You gain the trust and respect of your clients; they recognize the power of your recommendations; and you earn the right to ask for referrals.

Less Is More

How do you gain a reputation for your expertise? Sell more by narrowing your focus. For some salespeople, narrowing focus feels confining—as if they're leaving good business on the table. They often think that if they don't cast a wide net, they'll miss a sale. The opposite is true. The more specific you are, the more quickly you'll develop a reputation as the go-to expert in a particular industry or discipline.

How do you choose an expertise? Start by figuring out what you love about your favorite clients. For example, my friend George is an insurance agent who focuses exclusively on engineers. George studied engineering in school and loves working with numbers. He also loves working with engineers, because he understands their thought processes and knows exactly how to communicate with them.

The person who bought George's first policy offered to refer him to other engineers. He told his friends they had to talk to George, because George spoke their language. George quickly expanded his business, because the engineers viewed George as someone capable of explaining the complexities of insurance in a concrete, systematic manner. Thus, George became known as the go-to insurance provider for engineers.

How do you choose an expertise? Start by figuring out what you love about your favorite clients.

One of our family friends is a financial advisor who has made a great income by focusing exclusively on teachers. He has more than 20 years of experience in sales and has educated himself—through experience and research—on the financial needs of educators. Over time, he has earned the trust of many teachers, who continually refer their colleagues to him. He hasn't missed a sales award trip in decades.

You don't need or want just "any" business; you want the business that excites you and enables you to deliver solutions that actually help people. Can we all choose our perfect clients? You bet we can—whether we own a company or work for an enterprise—all thanks to the power of referrals. When we specialize and begin to cultivate expertise in a specific, targeted area where we have a personal interest or passion, we attract clients in that niche. And those people know (and refer) others just like themselves.

You Get What You Ask For

When it comes to new clients, focus on quality, not quantity.

Selling isn't like parenting. It's OK to have favorites. All salespeople recognize their ideal clients. You know who yours are. They value what you offer, communicate well, are forward thinking and reasonable, have a good sense of humor, and give you the time, money, and resources to make projects successful. With them, you close bigger deals faster. And they refer you to other ideal clients, saving you time on prospecting and shortening your sales cycle.

Selling isn't like parenting. It's OK to have favorites.

If a prospect doesn't fit your criteria for an ideal client, it's OK to walk away. "There are two winners in every sales deal," says Dawn Westerberg, founder of Dawn Westerberg Consulting. "There's the one who wins and the one who discovers early on that it's not the right deal and gets out." She says we often get so caught up in the frenzy of closing deals that we don't take the time to determine if prospects are the right fit for us. "We especially don't take into account the way our prospects treat the rest of the team. If someone doesn't share your beliefs, assumptions, and approach, that person shouldn't be your client."

As you're describing your ideal client to referral sources, be as specific as possible. Think of yourself as a sketch artist: The more color, lines, and detail you present, the easier it will be for them to recognize and identify your ideal client and refer the right people to you.

Thank You, Social Media

Social media is an invaluable tool for gaining a reputation as an expert in your field. Blogs, LinkedIn, Yahoo Answers!, and other online communities provide platforms to showcase our expertise. We learn what people are saying about us and our competitors, and what they need.

Brick-and-mortar establishments are about location, location, location. The cyber-world is about content, content, content. If you provide consistent, relevant, helpful content, and answer questions on your topic, you can quickly become known as the go-to expert for information on your industry, product/service, topic, etc.

The good news is that you don't always have to be the one who *creates* the content. Posting original content in a blog or on social media is certainly a valuable endeavor. But you can also be the *link* to valuable information.

Diane Updyke—the former vice president of sales for Crowd Factory, who currently serves as acting sales VP and advisor for several marketing and sales-intelligence companies—suggests finding interesting, relevant stories and articles online, and then sharing them with your social networks. "Educating the market gives you leverage," says Diane. "It puts you in a consultative role where you're providing clients and prospects with valuable information they might have otherwise missed."

Whether you post original content or share information from someone else, you're demonstrating that you've got your finger on the pulse of whatever is happening in your industry or area—which is what being an expert is all about.

If expertise is not specific and well-defined, you don't have expertise; you have a pastime. The faster you dip into your connections and interests, the faster clients and prospects will recognize you as an expert. Soon, fewer qualified leads will translate into more clients and more profitable business.

DELIVER THE PERSONAL CONNECTION

Computers do many things more effectively and efficiently than people, but outside of a few terrifying science-fiction movies, there's still one thing they can't do that we can, and that is *think* for ourselves.

Yes, I know a computer named Watson won the Jeopardy challenge in 2011.[8] But thinking is about more than just memorizing and regurgitating facts. While technology is great for storing, aggregating, and—to some degree—interpreting information, it can't have conversations, ask insightful questions, or draw wisdom from experience … at least not yet.

Russ Colombo, president and CEO of Bank of Marin, says, "Technology is a tool that can help us be more efficient, but it is not a substitute for talking to people."

I couldn't agree more. Technology expedites many tasks, but at the end of the day, people do business with people.

---

[8] "Watson," *Ask.com*, http://www.ask.com/wiki/Watson_%28computer%29 (last modified Aug. 19, 2013).

In fact, the more technology-driven this world gets, the more we appreciate actually talking to and working with *people.* John Naisbitt, author of *Megatrends* and several other international bestsellers, has explored this concept extensively over the last 40 years. In *High Tech/High Touch: Technology and Our Search for Meaning,*[9] he notes that while people like the excitement of high-tech—both the novelty as well as the rapid access to information—they don't like being treated like a number. He says: "The more high tech, the more high touch we desire."

The challenge, then, is to balance the high-tech innovation that drives today's business world with personal, high-touch relationships. It's not technology versus humanity, and it's not either/or. Consumers today want both. We're not changing the need for humanity, just some of the requirements.

Know Your Value

There's no replacement for the personal touch. In fact, people usually pay higher premiums to do business with those who provide exceptional service.

> It's not technology versus humanity, and it's not either/or. Consumers today want both.

Consider Nordstrom's reputation for customer service. Salespeople say hello, ask good questions, and come out from behind the counter to hand you your package. Nordstrom makes it easy to buy. You can purchase a pair of shoes and get one size for your right foot

[9] John Naisbitt, *High Tech/High Touch: Technology and Our Search for Meaning,* Broadway, 1999.

and another size for your left. And you can return purchased items (even those you've already worn) at any counter in the store, rather than standing in line at customer service.

Although Nordstrom's merchandise is a bit pricier than many other department stores, shoppers are willing to pay more for the good experience.

Starbucks is another great example. Millions of people around the world pay a premium for coffee at Starbucks when they could get their java from McDonald's for half the price, or just make a cup at home or work. But Starbucks offers more than coffee; it offers a variety of beverage options, a comfy atmosphere, and renowned customer service. A few years ago, the company shut down every U.S. location at the same time one evening to provide mandatory customer-service training for staff. They did this during business hours, sacrificing an evening's worth of profits (which, for a company of this size, is not a small chunk of change), because they understand that people don't pay more for their coffee because it's such an extraordinary product. Customers pay more for the *experience.*

These are both B2C examples, but the principles apply to B2B sales as well. During a recent referral program I hosted, we had a heated discussion about why price ceases to be an issue when you create value. One of the participants shared a story about hiring a new vendor at her previous company. She had narrowed it down to two companies. One salesperson spent time asking her question after question and offering solutions and advice. She connected with him immediately and felt confident that he understood her business and her concerns. The other vendor only talked about his company and his products. She chose the first vendor, even though he was more expensive. And she never regretted her decision.

People will pay more to work with reps they like and trust—salespeople who make them feel respected, heard, valued, and even a bit pampered. When you make it easy and pleasant to do business with you, you win clients for life.

People will pay more to work with reps they like and trust—salespeople who make them feel respected, heard, valued, and even a bit pampered.

Know Your ROI

Creating personal connections with our clients ensures we continue to provide value—and retain their business. If you're not talking to your clients on a fairly regular basis, how will you know if they're actually using your product and getting results?

If you sell software, you know the challenge. You sell one or two seats, or even a license. You get your commission, and all is well ... until renewal time, when you discover that the customer hasn't used your product or tapped into all of its functionality. Instead of getting an automatic renewal, you lose the client.

Equally important, you've missed the opportunity to ask this customer for a referral. You haven't stayed in touch, and the client hasn't gotten the expected ROI. Your sales cycle begins all over, and you're scrambling for new business when you could have had a loyal customer.

Know Your Customer

Craig Rosenberg, co-founder of TOPO, says technology gives us a faster, more efficient, better way to do the oldest sales fundamental—know the buyer.

I agree on the faster and better part, but how do buyers get to know us, and how do we get to know them? For that, you might just have to pick up the damn phone!

SECTION 2

IT'S STILL WHO YOU KNOW THAT COUNTS

When I interviewed Bill Binch, senior vice president of sales for Marketo, I expected to hear all about the advantages of marketing automation. Boy, was I wrong!

Instead, he talked about the power of relationships for sales. "It's not what you know," he told me. "It's who you know."

Bill's father was a salesman. At the end of a quarter, if his father needed one more deal to make quota, he would call in a favor from a buddy at XYZ company. "Dad would tell them that if they'd buy now, he would give them a great deal, so it would help both of them out. Selling was about two people connecting … and it still is."

When Bill was considering a new vendor, he spoke to a fellow VP at another company—a friend with whom he regularly meets to bounce around ideas. The two of them trust each other and value the relationship, so Bill didn't need to shop the market. He chose the vendor his friend recommended.

Bill is a founding member of The Silicon Valley VP of Sales Forum—a group of 80 to 100 sales executives in the Bay Area who meet every eight weeks to share ideas and best practices. Bill says the real value of this organization is the pre-session mingling, when members connect and bond over pizza and beer. While the purpose of the group is to share ideas, these VPs also share their networks. Bill has closed deals not only with other members of the forum, but also with people they referred to him.

"Relationships like this are how deals get done," says Bill. "When a trusted resource refers you to someone, you take the time to explore the option."

Marketing automation and CRM (which Bill considers a replacement for the Rolodex) are great tools for organizing the sales process. But at the end of the day, referrals are still the best way to generate qualified, hot leads with ideal clients.

What *will* give you an edge is a well-connected, well-nurtured network of people who are ready and willing to refer you.

Yes, you should have an online presence. You should utilize social media and explore the plethora of technology tools available to make your sales process more efficient. But don't fool yourself into thinking these tools give you a predictable, guaranteed edge, because everyone else is using the same tools.

What *will* give you an edge is a well-connected, well-nurtured network of people who are ready and willing to refer you. That's right—it's still who you know that counts.

To Know You Is to Like You

There's a saying in sales: Clients buy with emotion and justify with fact. If people don't like us and feel comfortable with us, they won't buy from us. You can wow prospects with your technological know-how up front and then try to win them over later, once they find out you're honest and reliable. But the reality is that you need people to start liking you within the first few seconds of your relationship.

Fancy gizmos and Facebook won't help you make a good impression. But a trusted referral and a personal connection will.

Fancy gizmos and Facebook won't help you make a good impression. But a trusted referral and a personal connection will. As Reid Hoffman, executive chairman and co-founder of LinkedIn, writes in his book, *The Start-Up of You,*[10] "When you reach out to someone via an introduction from a mutual friend, it's like having a passport at the border—you can walk right through. The interaction is immediately endowed with *trust*."

---

[10] Reid Hoffman and Ben Casnocha, *The Start-Up of You: Adapt to the Future, Invest in Yourself, and Transform Your Career,* Crown Business, 2012.

To Like You Is to Trust You

Building relationships takes time. That's why it's important to start demonstrating your trustworthiness right out of the gate. Evan Samurin, partner development manager for Infusionsoft, says, "Most salespeople don't take the time to develop relationships and build rapport at the beginning of a transaction. When customers know early on that you're going to diagnose the right solution and take care of them, it changes the scope of the interaction and builds trust."

How many times have you heard the phrase, "Trust me"? Uh, huh. Sure.

In an era of economic instability and wrecked public faith in business, trust is no longer the default starting point for skeptical consumers. That means salespeople must earn and nurture it over time. And we must deliver on trustworthiness every single day.

As Dawn Westerberg, founder of Dawn Westerberg Consulting, puts it, "We need to be deserving of a customer's trust. And we must constantly measure how our customers feel about our interactions." She adds that *conversation,* not technology, is the key to proving yourself worthy of their business. In fact, technology can be downright off-putting at times. "We are so overwhelmed with requests for electronic surveys; they seem to be as frequent as getting an oil change for your car. It's becoming as intrusive as telemarketing."

It takes time to earn our clients' trust, but when we invest in those relationships, we reap invaluable rewards.

Shake the Sales Rap

Sales has gotten a bad rap. Many buyers view us as pushy, arrogant, in-your-face people who only want the quick sale. They still picture the archetypal used-car salesman who flashes a big smile and talks a big game, and whom we're not certain we can trust.

This is not the kind of person you are. Truly great salespeople engender trust by:

- **Listening:** You have two ears and one mouth. Your conversation should be 80/20—with customers doing about 80 percent of the talking.

- **Validating:** Many customers feel that salespeople don't listen to them and don't understand the significance of their problems. Therefore, it's important to summarize what your clients say without sounding like you've just attended sales training and memorized a script (e.g., "So what I hear you saying is ...").

- **Offering solutions:** Great salespeople ask insightful questions, designed to help us understand exactly what our clients want and need, so we can offer the best possible solutions—even if that means referring them to someone better suited to help.

- **Caring:** If you do your work with other people's best interests in mind, and if your customers know you care about them, they will be loyal to you for years to come.

Great salespeople do right by their customers. They treat prospects and clients as they would want to be treated. And there's nothing pushy, sleazy, or "salesy" about that.

Trust and Technology

Ralf VonSosen, head of marketing and sales solutions for LinkedIn, says social media can help support our efforts to build trust earlier in the sales cycle—for several reasons. First, we can quickly find out if we have common relationships with key prospects—which, he says, is the most powerful way to build trust quickly. It also provides information about our prospects so we can have more insightful conversations. "The more meaningful conversations you can have," says Ralf, "the sooner you establish trust." Finally, your social-media profiles give you the opportunity to show up as a professional and to showcase recommendations and endorsements from people who have benefitted from your product or service.

One word of warning from Ralf (which I strongly second): "Social media enables you to have a meaningful conversation, to make that experience better—not to replace it."

"Social media enables you to have a meaningful conversation, to make that experience better—not to replace it."

To Trust You Paves the Way

When we've earned the trust of our clients, not only do they keep coming back for more (even bigger) deals, but they become our most loyal cheerleaders and advocates—spreading word of our value to their friends and colleagues. Relationships built on trust give us an edge over our competitors, who often don't even get a *chance* to compete. After all, why would our prospects bother shopping around if they already know they can trust us?

Trust trumps technology every day. Technology takes us just so far. Then it's time to make a personal connection!

Get Up Close and Personal

In his commencement address to the 2009 graduating class of the University of Pennsylvania, Eric Schmidt, executive chairman of Google, urged students to make human connections. "Turn off your computer," he said. "You're actually going to have to turn off your phone and discover all that is human around us."

In an era when companies cancel sales trips to cut costs, believing webcasts and videoconferences to be just as effective, they should be doing the opposite—scheduling more. Face-to-face meetings aren't luxuries. Even in our technology-driven world, nothing replaces a handshake and in-person interaction for both building and maintaining business relationships.

Face-to-face meetings aren't luxuries. Even in our technology-driven world, nothing replaces a handshake and in-person interaction for both building and maintaining business relationships.

In fact, 95 percent of business people agree that personal connections are the key to building long-term relationships, according to a *Harvard Business Review* reader poll. And according to the World Travel and

Tourism Council,[11] business travel improves corporate productivity, yielding a 10:1 return on investment.

Other key findings from this study:

- Global business travelers estimate that roughly 50 percent of their prospects are converted into clients with in-person meetings, compared to 31 percent without face time.

- On average, business travelers believe 38 percent of their customers would switch to a competitor, and that their companies would lose 37 percent of annual sales, without in-person meetings.

- Four out of five global executives (nine out of 10 in China) "agree" or "strongly agree" that face-to-face business meetings are essential to their organizations' success and that business travel improves a firm's chance of increasing sales.

Win the Numbers Game

One of my clients was working on a potential deal with a major prospect, but she couldn't get the decision-makers on the phone. I strongly recommended she schedule an in-person visit. Fast-forward two months. She not only met with potential buyers; she also made a presentation to 60 people and now has four strategic

---

[11] World Travel & Tourism Council, "Business Travel: A Catalyst for Economic Performance," http://www.wttc.org/site_media/uploads/downloads/WTTC_Business_Travel_2011.pdf (2011).

projects in the pipeline. Elated, she called me to say thank you. The personal visit sealed the deal.

One summer I tacked a 60-mile drive onto the end of a vacation to meet with a prospect. That business-development trip resulted in two speaking engagements—opportunities I would not have gotten without taking time to visit and build a new, mutually-respectful relationship.

You don't have to hop on an airplane. Drive your car; get on a bus; take a train. Just meet in person with every major client and prospect. You will accelerate your sales process by at least 30 percent, spend less time prospecting (who wouldn't want that?), and attract more quality clients.

Step away from the keyboard. The real world is waiting for you.

The Next Best Thing

Though it's ideal to meet in person, doing so is not always a realistic option with all of our clients—at least not frequently. So what counts as "face-to-face"? Any connection you make when you're not typing on your computer or smart phone.

Phone, video, in-person—they all count, but at different levels. If you can't meet in person, picking up the phone or connecting through video are close seconds. What's not even a close third, fourth, fifth, or 10th is emailing, texting, or sending a message via social media.

You Can't Have a Relationship with a Faceless Customer

I met Todd McCormick, senior vice president of sales for Silverpop, at a Sales 2.0 Conference in San Francisco. At the time, he was vice president of sales at PGi, a multinational video and teleconference company, and I was fascinated by his presentation on face-to-face meetings. I still remember him saying how important it is to see "the whites of their eyes."

Todd says research shows that most consumers like being loyal. In fact, one study found that four out of five people prefer *not* to shop around. And yet, in a *Harvard Business Review* study,[12] 60 percent of buyers reported switching providers—even when they were happy with their current vendors' service. Why?

As Todd explains in his blog post,[13] "You may not think of your prospects or customers as merely a number that brings you closer to quota, but they can easily feel like it if you don't get face to face on a frequent basis. If you want customers to stick around, you need to let them see you."

> If you can't meet in person, picking up the phone or connecting through video are close seconds. What's not even a close third, fourth, fifth, or 10th is emailing, texting, or sending a message via social media.

Just as importantly, *you* need to see *them*. As Todd puts it, "When you limit communication to email and telephone, you miss out on one of the most important aspects of closing the sale: Nonverbal communication."

Webcam Wisdom

Many sales professionals are correcting this problem by tapping into the selling power of nonverbal communication through online

---

[12] Scott Robinette, "Get Emotional," *Harvard Business Review*, http://hbr.org/2001/05/get-emotional/ar/1 (May 2001).

[13] Todd McCormick, "You Can't Have a Relationship with a Faceless Customer," *PGI*, http://blog.pgi.com/2012/07/you-cant-have-a-relationship-with-a-faceless-customer/ (July 24, 2012).

meetings and video chats. In fact, some experts say these options can be even more effective than in-person meetings, because the close-up view that webcams provide forces us to focus on the important source of nonverbal communication: Facial expression.

Video conferencing is a great way to get face to face with clients. But while it may be as close as you can get to in-person, it's not, and you're not. If you have a big-deal prospect or client, you'd better jump on a plane, catch a train, or take a road trip as soon as possible. Your competition is probably still fooling around with technology.

Out of Sight, Out of Mind: Connecting Your Virtual Team

Our clients aren't the only ones with whom we have virtual relationships. Many companies have teams of people working together, who have never been in the same room. And that's too bad, because there's nothing like getting the gang together.

Salespeople have great combined power and energy when they gather in person and share successes, sales techniques, ideas, and information. At conferences we learn as much through conversations with peers in the hallways as we do in our sessions. But there's no "hallway" on the World Wide Web. And there's no water cooler around which your virtual employees can gather to shoot the breeze, or to put their heads together and solve a problem.

Heads in the Cloud

This is a new era in business culture—the rise of the Cloud Collar Worker.[14] Technology has not only changed how we work but also

---

[14] Blakely Thomas-Aguilar, "Are Cloud Collar Workers the Future of Work?," *PGI*, http://blog.pgi.com/2012/11/are-cloud-collar-workers-the-future-of-work/ (Nov. 12, 2012).

the nature of our work. There are now more than 600 million people who are part of an emerging (and rapidly-growing) group called "information workers"—meaning they specialize in information, not production. This labor force will grow to more than 865 million workers by 2016, according to Forrester Research.[15]

The Value of Virtual Workers

Cindy Bates, vice president of U.S. SMB and distribution for Microsoft, says the cloud enables companies to shrink their sales cycles and dramatically reduce operating costs—in part, by making it easier than ever to have virtual workforces. Thanks to cloud-based software, tablets, and smart phones, we can access data anywhere, anytime, and can stay connected to colleagues, customers, and suppliers.

> There's no water cooler around which your virtual employees can gather to shoot the breeze, or to put their heads together and solve a problem.

Cindy told me about the owner of a consulting firm, who was on the road so much he decided to get rid of his office space and have his 65 employees work remotely. By doing so, he has saved $1 million in overhead costs.

The cost-effectiveness of virtual workforces has made it a fast-growing trend. The number of telecommuters in the U.S. has

---

[15] Forrester Research, Inc., "Info Workers Will Erase the Boundary Between Enterprise and Consumer Technologies," 2013.

increased by 800 percent in the past five years, according to Nemertes Research. And experts say that number will keep growing.

However, the more virtual our workforces become, the more we lose the personal connectivity and spirit of teamwork that makes a company great.

Get the Gang Together

I have a virtual team, but I get everyone in the same room at least twice a year. We discuss what's working, what's not, and what's new. Sometimes we even argue, and ultimately we plan our sales and marketing strategies for the coming months.

We also have a casual holiday lunch each year—where we feast on burgers, sweet-potato fries, and milkshakes (and maybe even beer). It's not fancy, but the cost of the meal is not what people appreciate. They appreciate the opportunity to spend time together.

After receiving my holiday lunch invitation, one team member sent me the following note: "I just wanted to say thank you for doing this. Working with you is a genuine treat, and it's the extra-mile stuff that makes [our team] feel like a family. Looking forward to seeing everyone."

I have worked with this person for more than six years. He used to come to my office once a month, but now he works virtually. He's a Millennial (a generation notorious for relying too heavily on technology for communication), but he still sees the value in getting together.

Whether we're talking about clients, prospects, or even our own teams, the lesson still applies: Technology is great, but human beings are too social a species to rely solely on electronic communication. We need to spend time with other people—not just our computers.

Word of the Decade: Collaboration

Collaboration is the word of the second decade of the 21st century (2011-2020). That's according to Barry Trailer, managing partner of CSO Insights. But collaborating is as old as time. Bartering is a form of collaboration, and so are negotiation and teamwork. Collaboration leads to entrepreneurship, which leads to innovation.

According to Stephen Spinelli and Rob Adams, authors of *New Venture Creation,*[16] 95 percent of all radical innovation since World War II has come from small firms—typically companies created by a series of collaborative ventures.

So why is collaboration suddenly the new buzz word?

Globalization

At last, business people realize we live in a global economy. We appreciate the unique perspectives that diverse individuals bring to the table. As a colleague once told me, there is a difference

---

[16] Stephen Spinelli and Rob Adams, *New Venture Creation: Entrepreneurship for the 21st Century*, McGraw-Hill-Irwin, 2011.

between an international company—one with offices around the world—and a global company. Global means the ability to work across borders, to understand and communicate with different cultures, and to build teams that work hand-in-hand with clients.

Mike Hurst, a partner at HurstWorks Consulting and a colleague of mine in the National Speakers Association, delivered a presentation entitled "The Language of Business," in which he reminded the audience that "just because we speak English, doesn't mean we are understood."

For example, during a presentation in Sao Paulo, Brazil, Mike used a gesture that has an affirmative meaning in the U.S. but is considered derogatory in Brazil. He also referred to the U.S. as "America," and his audience quickly corrected him, reminding him that Brazil is also part of America, just not the *United States* of America.

There's been a long-standing joke between those of us in the U.S. and people "across the pond" in the U.K. that the only thing separating us is our language. We have many different expressions and colloquialisms. I often have to ask my British friends for clarification, and vice versa.

While visiting cousins in Manchester, England, I tried my best to stay awake through dinner, but I'd just taken a 12-hour flight and was suffering from jet lag. Finally I had to excuse myself. "I'm going to wash up," I said. "I'll see you in the morning." The next day my husband told me that, after I left the table, my cousin asked, "Why is Joanne washing up? We already did the dishes." Same words, two different meanings.

It's easy to ask our friends "What the heck does that mean?"—but not so easy to ask in a business situation.

Financial Hardship

The global recession of 2008–2010 forced us to work differently. Phones stopped ringing; requests for proposals diminished; and companies laid off seasoned workers. Many of these veterans took the opportunity to start their own companies. As they explored different growth strategies, they began reaching out to and collaborating with other entrepreneurs. They had conversations that never would have occurred in a vibrant economy. I received calls and emails from a variety of people and companies suggesting ways to work together and asking how we could help each other. Everyone explored creative ideas, and companies formed exciting alliances.

Software companies have talked about collaboration for years, but it was pretty much just hot air until the recession. Then they realized that some business is better than no business, that collaborating with other vendors makes every sales organization stronger, and that doing so enables companies to deliver the best products to customers. Do these collaborations always work? Of course not. But at least business leaders are getting over their fear of sharing knowledge and warming up to the idea of exploring collaborative sales strategies.

Technology

Cloud computing empowers collaboration on a greater scale than ever before. And thanks to social media, Skype, and other Web tools, geographically-distributed sales teams can now quickly access information (and each other) from anywhere, on any device. We can tap into best practices and team selling, meet with clients, brainstorm with partners, and negotiate deals—all from different continents if necessary.

The Lone Ranger Rides No More

George Papa, senior vice president of worldwide sales for Altera Corporation, says that in the past, when he was calling on accounts, he could walk in the client's front door, and all the decisions would be made under one roof. "Today a system is built in one part of the world, implemented in another, and marketed in another," he says. "We need to understand the needs and wants of people around the globe. The selling process becomes more complex, and those who can work as a team and share data will be successful."

Salespeople of old were mostly lone rangers. They viewed data as power and didn't share information. They had their zip codes to call on, and they did so alone. Now salespeople often depend on getting relevant client information from employees in multiple locations around the globe. This means we must be able to trust our teammates, and they need to trust us. When we share data, account strategies, and best practices with our colleagues, everyone wins bigger—including the client, who gets a better solution. George continues: "If you work as a lone ranger, you might close a million-dollar deal. But if you work as a global team, that could be a 20 million-dollar deal."

Team Players Only

George says the key to creating a collaborative environment is having a sales force made up of team players. He has made great progress at Altera in building trust and sharing successes. Because his management team members have lived and worked in many parts of the world, they understand cultural and social differences. Employees in each geography are hungry to learn, which makes them more willing to work (and grow) together.

It's always people who make the difference, says George, even in an analytical company like Altera. "If you get the wrong people in the right boxes, your organization will never work. If you get the wrong boxes and the right people, it will always work." In other words, having the right people is what's most important; getting them in the right roles is secondary.

George makes a good point, but if sales leaders don't set clear goals for their teams and create environments where teamwork is rewarded, people will never trust each other, let alone collaborate. George created a cohesive team—not only because he hired the right people, but because his management style supports, recognizes, and encourages collaboration. (George didn't say that. It's my perspective. He's a great guy—an expert in his field who values collaboration and knows how to laugh.)

> If sales leaders don't set clear goals for their teams and create environments where teamwork is rewarded, people will never trust each other, let alone collaborate.

Collaborate with Your Competition?

Donal Daly, founder and CEO of The TAS Group, is the brains behind Dealmaker Genius—an intelligent system that automates the creation of sales processes. He told me about collaborating in an online group at SalesEdgeOne, which brought together experts from his field to share ideas about improving life for sales professionals around the world.

Knowledge is no longer power. Collaboration is the new power equation.

This is a classic example of many heads being better than one. "When others play in your world, everyone's experience is enriched," he says. "You choose your friends, and they choose you. How you unselfishly put your virtual heads together as true allies in pursuit of a common objective will impact whether the friendships endure."

Play Nice or Go Home

In today's business world, identifying ways to work collaboratively with internal teams, vendors, and customers is what sets you apart. You can keep playing the lone ranger if you want, but don't expect the kind of results your team-playing colleagues are getting.

Knowledge is no longer power. Collaboration is the new power equation.

Social Networking Isn't "Social" Enough

As Woody Allen famously said, "Eighty percent of success is showing up." Showing up counts. So does being present and contributing. We show up in many different ways—online, offline, at work, with family, with friends, when volunteering, and even when working out. Showing up means you become involved. You contribute, you begin a task, and you take action. The more often you show up, the more visible you become, and the more people get to know, recognize, and respect you.

That's why networking is critical to building a solid base of referral sources. Thankfully, there are plenty of opportunities to develop and manage your referral network. And while social media can help you stay connected, *making connections* means doing some networking the old-fashioned way—offline.

Network Before You Need It

When I tell clients I expect them to attend at least one business networking event each week in order to generate new referral sources, they complain about not having enough time. But for salespeople, I can't think of a more important way to spend time than meeting new people and building relationships.

Every new person with whom you connect could be a potential client or referral source. Networking means talking to people, building relationships, and being genuine. As a sales professional, you're probably already good at those things.

Networking opportunities exist everywhere—meetings, professional associations, alumni groups, sports teams, conferences, community groups, weddings, parties, and any place people come together. So get out there. Go where your clients go. Join organizations. Make the time.

Spread the Wealth

Every association needs and welcomes volunteers in all shapes and sizes. Think about ways to contribute—whether you have the skill set to sit on a nonprofit board or could help out in other ways. When you volunteer, people learn how you work, that you are dependable and innovative, and that you deliver what you promise. Working with others for a good cause helps you develop strong, trusting relationships with people who *want* to do business with you and who will refer their networks.

Networking means talking to people, building relationships, and being genuine. As a sales professional, you're probably already good at those things.

Another great way to build your network is to help other people build theirs. John Tellenbach, senior vice president at Comerica Bank, has a "two by two" rule. His bankers want connections with CPAs, but in the past, they would meet with 20 CPAs and get no results. Now his bankers invite another person along for meetings—someone with whom the CPA would want to be connected, such as a corporate attorney or a mergers-and-acquisition resource. "This interaction primes the pump," John says. "Instead of coming with your hands open, you are saying that you can add value to their book of business." Now, instead of a 20:1 return, his bankers have better than a 5:1 return with CPAs.

In his book, *The Start-Up of You,*[17] LinkedIn's executive chairman and co-founder Reid Hoffman says the best way to strengthen a relationship is to ask how you can help another person. "The second best way is to let yourself be helped. As Ben Franklin recommended, 'If you want to make a friend, let someone do you a favor.'"

Stop Eating at Your Desk

A managing partner in a CPA firm once told me he was amazed that people in his office sat at their desks all day—even at lunch. So he gave his sales team a challenge—four breakfasts and five lunches every week. That's nine meetings a week. It could be 10, he said, but no one wants to meet for breakfast on a Monday morning.

Nine meetings a week equals roughly 36 meetings a month. Subtracting four weeks a year for vacation and travel, that's 396 meetings a year. Do his sales reps reach that goal? Rarely. But to grow, you need a goal, so why not aim high?

To bring new clients to your company, your most important business-development activity is expanding your referral network. Even if you meet with only 200 referral sources each year, and only half of them introduce you to potential clients, you still have 100 hot leads.

---

[17] Reid Hoffman and Ben Casnocha, *The Start-Up of You: Adapt to the Future, Invest in Yourself, and Transform Your Career,* Crown Business, 2012.

Yes, showing up counts. And so does continuing to reach out and stay in touch with the people in your networks—especially when you don't want or need anything from them.

Nurture Your Network

You know those people who only reach out when they want something—the people who drop off the face of the earth until they need a referral, who forget all about you until they want an introduction to someone in your network. After a while, don't you find yourself thinking, "But what have *you* done for *me* lately?"

You don't want to be one of those people, but it's easy to get so caught up in developing new relationships that we forget about the existing ones ... until we need something from them. Big mistake!

Your goal as a salesperson is to build *and maintain* many strong relationships. That means nurturing those contacts, even after they no longer seem useful. Make it a daily discipline to connect with people in your networks—personal and professional. And by "connect," I don't mean send a vague, generic email. Use social channels to find out what's going on with them. Then pick up the phone and *talk*.

It's important to stay in touch with other salespeople, colleagues (past and present), and anyone else within our professional circles. But the most important relationships to nurture are those with current clients—not only because doing so helps us keep their business, but because they are best positioned to refer more great clients. After all, who knows our value better than those who have received a measurable ROI from our products and solutions?

Whatever you do, keep nurturing those relationships. Take your current clients to breakfast or lunch, or just out for coffee or drinks—with no agenda except to catch up and chat about how you can help each other. If they're not local, schedule video conferences. Just get face to face.

Tee up the conversation in one of two ways:

Once you've done the groundwork to earn someone's trust and friendship, don't waste that effort by neglecting to stay in touch until you want something.

- Find out how you can help them.
- Discover how you can help each other.

It's amazing what happens at these informal meetings. Your clients might not know the full range of services you provide or who would be an ideal referral for you—until you spend a little time building a relationship and discussing how you can support each other.

Bank of Marin's Russ Colombo says relationships are what set his organization apart from the big banks. "Selling is still a personal business. You need to know your customers, and they need to know you. We pose insightful questions and don't talk about the bank. People love to talk about themselves."

Most of Russ's clients still come from referrals—which, he points out, is very much a two-way street. That's why he trains his lenders to ask for referrals *and* to look for opportunities to provide them.

Selling is all about building relationships. Once you've done the groundwork to earn someone's trust and friendship, don't waste that effort by neglecting to stay in touch until you want something.

Make nurturing relationships a priority. When people in your network have big events—product launches, speaking events, or even something major in their personal lives—send congratulatory notes and wish them luck. If your company has a big deadline looming for a client, make a note of that in your calendar so you can check in and make sure everything is on track.

Just keep reaching out and preserving your most valuable sales asset—your relationships.

SECTION 3

SOCIAL MEDIA: YOU'RE THE NEXT BIG THING

Social networking isn't the next big thing. You are!

It's not technology, but rather the person behind the technology, that sets you apart. You have a conversation and you share a comment, a reply, a laugh, or a shared interest. It's emotional! And it has the power to give your business a personality when you thought that wasn't possible.

The Internet, social networking, smart phones, and other technological breakthroughs have fundamentally changed the way we do business. New technology drives communications, messaging, and information access at warp speed, and our clients expect immediate access. This pattern of ever-increasing sophistication not only creates an intensely-competitive marketplace; it also places further demands on us to act and react quickly.

Social-networking sites such as LinkedIn, Facebook, Twitter, YouTube, and Pinterest (and the many others that seem to surface hourly) lure many sales pros into scaling back their sometimes time-consuming personal interactions and relying on social media to surface easy "qualified" leads. Big mistake!

Get Real

Social media is a powerful and valuable sales tool. But it serves these purposes only:

1. Researching new or potential clients
2. Learning more about the networks of those in your social networks
3. Identifying the strongest connections to your hot prospects
4. Building a community of loyal customers
5. Positioning yourself as an expert
6. Search engine optimization

Some salespeople tell me they actually attract new clients through social media. Could it happen? Yes. Would I rely on it? Absolutely not. I only count on what I bring about—through a proactive and intentional referral-selling strategy with personal introductions.

Let's zero-in on how social media has (and hasn't) changed the sales game, how to make it work for you, how to leverage your connections for referral introductions, and how to get the most out of your LinkedIn profile.

Some salespeople tell me they actually attract new clients through social media. Could it happen? Yes. Would I rely on it? Absolutely not.

Has Social Media Changed the Way We Sell?

It often seems that social media has changed everything about our society. People turn to social-networking sites for everything from entertainment, to news, to advice on buying decisions, to finding a romantic partner (another kind of prospecting). Some engaged couples even use social media in lieu of wedding invitations (probably causing poor Emily Post to roll over in her grave).

Social media has definitely changed some things. But has it changed the way we sell? Yes and no.

Social selling enables us to more effectively gather information, conduct research, and identify connections. And it definitely impacts the early stages of our sales processes, enabling us to quickly assess a buyer's qualifications and spend less time on unproductive prospecting.

However, it has *not* changed the way we talk to prospects, how buyers relate to us, and why they choose us over our competition. Top salespeople understand that selling requires building strong relationships with our clients—relationships based on mutual respect and trust. And with few exceptions, this cannot be done online, especially if you're targeting high-level decision-makers.

Decision-Makers Don't Do Facebook

Jonathan Farrington, CEO of JF Consultancy, says that while social media has changed the way we sell in certain sectors, "it's not the be-all, end-all." And he's fearful that younger generations of salespeople don't understand that. He explains, "They think, 'Let's write a blog and be active on Twitter, LinkedIn, and Facebook, and we're bound to find all the clients we could possibly need.' But that's not enough."

The problem, Jonathan says, is that high-level decision makers—you know, the people who can green-light the really big deals—aren't spending much time on social media.

> Top salespeople understand that selling requires building strong relationships with our clients—relationships based on mutual respect and trust. And with few exceptions, this cannot be done online, especially if you're targeting high-level decision-makers.

Jeff Rosenthal, a senior partner for Korn/Ferry Leadership and Talent Consulting Business, echoes Jonathan's sentiment: "The more senior the decision-maker, the less active he or she is on social media. It's a distraction they don't want to bother with. They have enough people badgering them and asking for things."

Though LinkedIn's research shows that nine out of 10 executives use LinkedIn at least once a week, IBM's 2012 Global CEO Study shows that only 16 percent of CEOs participate in social media.[18] And among the CEOs of Fortune-500 companies, 70 percent aren't active on any social-media sites, according to CEO.com and Domo.[19]

This is exactly why relationships still rule in sales. Senior leaders might not be active on social media, but they *will* take calls from people they know, trust, and like. According to a study of 125 senior executives by Responsibility Centered Leadership,[20] the top two reasons they take meetings with salespeople are when they receive a recommendation from a credible source within their organizations, or when they receive an external referral from a respected source.

But Don't Delete Your Profile Just Yet

All of this is not to say that social media is useless to salespeople. On the contrary, it can be a powerful tool—for *gathering information.*

Donal Daly, CEO and founder of The TAS Group, offers an interesting perspective:

> Social Media and SCRM (Social CRM) are new, but what 'social' represents in both of these terms is as old as selling. It means understanding what's important to our customers, from both a personal and corporate

---

[18] IBM, "Insights from the IBM Global CEO Study," http://www-935.ibm.com/services/us/en/c-suite/ceostudy2012/ (2012).

[19] "2012 CEO.com Social CEO Report." CEO.com and Domo, http://www.domo.com/news/press-releases/fortune-500-ceos-are-shunning-social-media-says-new-study-by-domo-and-ceo-com (2012).

[20] Kent J. Gregoire, "Selling at the Executive Level: A summary of studies examining how client executives view their relationships with professional salespeople," Responsibility Centered Leadership, 2011.

> perspective—and engaging with them in terms they are familiar with, and about topics that are uppermost in their minds. Empathy is at the heart of selling. To empathize, you must first understand, and before understanding comes knowledge.

Daly concludes that it's too early to have proven, established best practices in the Social Universe, and that to say otherwise means denying the pace of change. According to him, "It's not that long ago since Twitter didn't exist, and every day other new paradigms are emerging. The best we can do is to observe, engage and learn, and then try something."

I completely agree. Though 54 percent of salespeople can track closed deals back to social media,[21] the impact of social media on sales results is still hotly debated.

Social media plays a critical role in our sales efforts. But use it wisely. Remember, you're still the star of the show.

---

[21] Barbara Giamanco and Jim Keenan, "Social Media and Sales Quota: The Impact of Social Media on Sales Quota and Corporate Revenue," A Sales Guy Consulting and Social Centered Selling, 2013.

Put Social Media to Work for You

Social media is an invaluable tool for sales, but it hasn't changed the way we build relationships. It *has,* however, given us access to information that can help us conduct "business as usual" more effectively and efficiently—as long as we understand the parameters.

As marketing keynote speaker and bestselling author Jay Baer puts it:

> People tell you all the time that social media is a conversation between brands and customers, and that's not really true. Social media isn't a conversation. Social media is where the conversation takes place. Just showing up to social media doesn't really count for anything. It's what you do with social media that counts, not the fact that you just show up to the party.

So what do you do once you've shown up to the party? Use social media in the six ways we discussed:

1. Researching new or potential clients

2. Learning more about the networks of the people you know

3. Identifying the strongest connections to your hot prospects

4. Building a community of loyal customers

5. Positioning yourself as an expert

6. Search engine optimization

I'm not the only one who thinks this is true. In every interview I conducted for this book, I asked business leaders how social media has effectively changed the sales game. Across the board, they pointed to these six ways.

Do Your Research

In the age of social media and Google, prospects expect you to know as much as possible about them and their companies. Craig Rosenberg, co-founder of TOPO, says, "Buyers today are busier than ever. When they know you've done the work, they are more willing to accept a conversation with you."

Many of the leaders I interviewed for this book told me they won't have anything to do with salespeople who haven't done their homework before the initial meeting. This is where social media proves especially useful. Research is the No. 1 way in which salespeople use LinkedIn.[22] And 61.4 percent of those who do so say it makes them more successful at initiating conversations with prospects.

Research is about more than proving to prospects that you're taking their business seriously. It's also about finding ways to

---

[22] Jill Konrath and Ardath Albee, *Cracking the LinkedIn Code*, http://www.jillkonrath.com/linkedin-sales-code/ (2013).

connect—to learn about their interests and what you have in common so that you have something to talk about other than business and the weather.

Jill Rowley, social selling evangelist at Oracle, says that strategic use of social media has helped her close many deals. For example, when she got a notification that a VP had clicked through her email about why CMOs should carry a quota, she went to LinkedIn and read his profile. Upon discovering they both attended the University of Virginia, she sent him a personal note with "Go Wahoos!" in the subject line. She got a response within 30 minutes. They started to communicate, and she received an RFP shortly after, thus beginning a business relationship that never would have happened without social-media interaction and follow-up (and, I'll add, *creativity*).

> Research is about more than proving to prospects that you're taking their business seriously. It's also about finding ways to connect.

Who Knows Whom?

Quality referrals can come from the most unexpected sources, and often the people we write off, certain they don't know anyone who might be helpful to our businesses, are somehow connected to exactly the decision-makers we want to meet.

Jill Rowley says there's new math: One plus one equals three. That's why she researches the connections of everyone she meets. For example, whenever she gets member directories for her daughters' athletic teams, she looks up the other players' parents on LinkedIn to see if there might be a business opportunity. One of these parents happened to be an executive at her client company. Understanding the importance of getting executive buy-in, she mentioned that their daughters were on the same team, connected with him after the next practice, and subsequently initiated a business conversation.

Get HOT Prospects

Let's say there's a particular client you've been dying to win over, but you can't even get your foot in the door—or, at least, not into the corner office where it counts. What do you need to get past the dreaded gatekeeper and into the high-level meeting you want to have? That's right—a referral from someone that decision-maker trusts. Before social media, you might have spent weeks making calls, asking everyone in your network, "Do you know anyone influential at DoNotCall Corp?"

Now finding possible referral sources is as easy as logging into LinkedIn, searching your contacts for someone connected to your prospect, and then asking for an introduction.

Engage Your Customers

Social sites can also be a great way to connect your customers to one another—or to other people who can provide them with value.

Social sites can also be a great way to connect your customers to one another—or to other people who can provide them with value.

Microsoft did this by creating a marketing match-up on Facebook, connecting partners with customers who had technology questions. Within a month of the launch, 6,000 customers came to the site and engaged with partners on technology questions—earning Microsoft the gratitude of every consumer who used the platform to get answers.

Many companies form online communities where customers share information and provide answers to technical and strategic questions. They value hearing from people "who've done it" more than hearing from a salesperson or account manager. There are now more than 2.1 million LinkedIn Groups,[23] where members can collaborate and ask and answer questions. I've created a private LinkedIn group for participants in my Referral Selling Masters Program. I post short articles. People respond and ask questions that are urgent for them. There is great power in group wisdom and the give and take of people with similar interests.

David Novak, executive vice president of sales and business development for SPS Commerce, suggests using social media to connect your clients with each other—enabling them to get contacts, information, and referrals through your company. "Talk about paying it forward," he says. "New networked businesses are about transacting between partners." His trading-partner directory includes representatives from 40,000 companies—all of whom can talk to each other and look for opportunities to do business together.

You're the Expert

Your social-media profiles are not the place to promote your company. That's what your corporate website is for. Instead, use social sites to provide value—interesting, thoughtful, helpful, educational content. As Dan Druker, chief marketing officer for MyBuys, puts it, "If you're not sharing your expertise, you're wasting peoples' time."

---

[23]As of August 2013. *LinkedIn*, http://press.linkedin.com/about/.

Who's Looking for You?

Social media enables you to increase your Web presence. By populating your profiles and blog with your keywords and with links to and from your website, you get more love (i.e., a higher ranking) from search engines.

Kurt Shaver, founder of the Sales Foundry, says that a major component of SEO is the volume of what you pump out. The more individuals on a sales force who post, the better the company's SEO will be. For example, HubSpot—an inbound marketing company—requires all new salespeople to blog. "These blogs can be on any subject the employees want to discuss," Kurt says. "The key is to build an audience." This not only helps salespeople become experts when they talk on the phone to clients, but it also drives HubSpot's SEO. "They have hundreds of people doing tiny contributions, which in aggregate, becomes a very big deal."

That's All, Folks

Social media certainly makes it easier to gather information about our prospects and to provide them with valuable information about us and our areas of expertise. In fact, when sales reps use the right social-selling approach, they are 25 to 50 percent more likely to get in front of prospects.[24] And 78 percent of salespeople using social media outsell their peers.

For the record: If you're not in play in social media, you're not in business. But after you've done your homework, it's time to log

---

[24] Barbara Giamanco and Jim Keenan, "Social Media and Sales Quota: The Impact of Social Media on Sales Quota and Corporate Revenue," A Sales Guy Consulting and Social Centered Selling, 2013.

off and rely on your relationship-building skills to get you the introduction, secure a meeting at the level that counts, and seal the deal.

Get Linked In

With more than 238 million members in more than 200 countries and territories,[25] LinkedIn is the world's largest online network of professionals. In fact, professionals are signing up to join LinkedIn at a rate of more than two new members per second. Facebook and Twitter have considerably more users, but for business purposes, LinkedIn is the best place to learn about prospects—including their current employers, where they used to work, where they went to school, their interests and travels, and how we're connected to them through mutual association.

LinkedIn's data shows that sales professionals experience a B2B conversion rate that's four times better than with Facebook or Twitter. And buyers are 50 percent more likely to purchase from a vendor with whom they've engaged on LinkedIn.

Clients *expect* to be able to find us on LinkedIn. But many sales professionals have yet to figure out just how to leverage this valuable resource.

Jill Konrath, author of *SNAP Selling*,[26] surveyed 3,094 salespeople about how using LinkedIn has translated into sales opportunities. Her findings: Only 4.9 percent of respondents have created "lots"

---

[25] As of September, 2013. *LinkedIn*, http://press.linkedin.com/About.
[26] Jill Konrath, *SNAP Selling: Speed Up Sales and Win More Business with Today's Frazzled Customers,* Portfolio Trade, 2012.

of opportunities, and 39.4 percent have created "several."[27] However, 55.5 percent still have "never" had a business opportunity they can attribute to LinkedIn.

"Many salespeople don't have a clue how to get started," says Jill. Even when opportunities were generated, 44.6 percent of those who benefited said their biggest challenge was not knowing how to use what's available from LinkedIn. Of all respondents, 58 percent said they don't understand LinkedIn's capabilities, and 41.2 percent lacked the time to learn/use it effectively.

However, Jill says salespeople who learn how to unlock LinkedIn's potential reap the rewards. "Those who have embraced it as a growth strategy are leveraging the tool to get business they never would have had. They're checking everything out, looking for hooks to create human, not just business, connections."

> Clients *expect* to be able to find us on LinkedIn. But many sales professionals have yet to figure out just how to leverage this valuable resource.

So how do you create those human connections that make LinkedIn so valuable?

Sell Yourself

People don't visit your LinkedIn profile to learn everything about your company. They want to learn more about *you*. They want

---

[27] Jill Konrath and Ardath Albee, *Cracking the LinkedIn Code*, http://www.jillkonrath.com/linkedin-sales-code/, 2013

to see a picture of *you*—one that reflects your personality and professionalism—not your company's logo.

Eric Blumthal, CEO of Count 5, suggests using the same headshot on your website and all of your social profiles. For most people, faces are easier to remember than names. Eric started out using different images across different platforms, but once he committed to just one, people from his Twitter account began to recognize him and reach out on LinkedIn.

As you're creating your profile, keep your audience in mind. Jill Konrath warns that because prospects will check you out on LinkedIn, you want to create a customer-centric profile, not an online résumé. "Your prospects would cringe if they read that you're an aggressive salesperson who has achieved quota for the past seven years," she says. Instead, highlight the value you have provided to former clients and the results they got as a result of working with you.

> People don't visit your LinkedIn profile to learn everything about your company. They want to learn more about *you.*

Personalize It

With all its automated messages, LinkedIn makes it easy to get lazy. When you invite someone into your network, don't just use the standard request (i.e., "I'd like to add you to my professional network on LinkedIn"). Tell *why* you want to connect. Perhaps you attended a webinar this person conducted, followed a discussion, met at an event, or used to work together.

Nurture your LinkedIn connections by offering to help—even when you haven't been asked and when you don't have a request to make.

LinkedIn also provides the option for automated introduction requests. Big mistake! People I respect tell me that when they receive automated requests for introductions, they feel imposed upon. And those messages are easy to ignore without feeling too guilty.

When you get ready to ask a referral source for an introduction to a prospect, reach out personally (preferably via phone or in person). Not only does this give you the opportunity to check in and nurture the relationship, but you also learn if your referral source actually knows your prospect. Many people accept every LinkedIn invitation, even those from people they don't know.

Give to Receive

Nurture your LinkedIn connections by offering to help—even when you haven't been asked and when you don't have a request to make. Two people recently reached out to me on LinkedIn, their only goal being to build connections, share wisdom, and learn about each other.

In one instance, someone I didn't recognize but who knew me as a referral-selling expert sent the following message, introducing me to a man named Jack:

> Going through my contacts, it occurs to me that the two of you are some of the most highly-connected people I know, and that's reason enough to introduce you. I have no idea where you might overlap business-

> wise, but with the staggering number of connections between you, there must be an opportunity there somewhere.

Jack and I set up a call. We shared stories and points of view, and we truly liked each other by the end of our discussion. We agreed to stay in touch, knowing we would collaborate somehow in the future. Soon after, he introduced me to Rodger, who immediately connected me with decision-makers at his company and offered to refer me to some of his clients (before I even had the chance to ask). And this was all on our first call!

I invite you to connect with me on LinkedIn if you think doing so would be valuable to both of us. Be sure to let me know who you are and why you'd like to connect. After all, when you build your business through referrals, you can never have too many relationships.

Too Many Friends?

I am not one of those people who attempts to connect with random strangers on social media, nor do I accept every friend request that comes my way (except from those who explain *why* they want to connect). That being said, I'm eager to meet new people—online and off. After all, the more people I know, the bigger my referral network grows.

In recent years, there's been an ongoing debate about the value of meaningful connections versus weak ones. One leader in this discussion is evolutionary psychologist Robin Dunbar, who discovered what many believe to be the magic number of relationships—150.

As *Businessweek* writer Drake Bennett summarizes:[28]

> In the same way that human beings can't breathe underwater or run the 100-meter dash in 2.5 seconds or see microwaves with the naked eye, most cannot maintain many more than 150 meaningful relationships. Cognitively, we're just not built for it … [O]nce a group grows larger than 150, its members begin to lose

[28] Drake Bennett, "The Dunbar Number, from the Guru of Social Networks," *Bloomberg Business Week*, http://www.businessweek.com/articles/2013-01-10/the-dunbar-number-from-the-guru-of-social-networks#p1.

> their sense of connection. … "The figure of 150 seems to represent the maximum number of individuals with whom we can have a genuinely social relationship, the kind of relationship that goes with knowing who they are and how they relate to us," Dunbar has written. "Putting it another way, it's the number of people you would not feel embarrassed about joining uninvited for a drink if you happened to bump into them in a bar."

On the other hand, as Morten Hansen points out in his book, *Collaboration*,[29] meaningful relationships aren't the only rewarding connections. Weaker ties can be just as valuable. In fact, one of Hansen's networking rules is to "build weak ties, not strong ones."

According to Hansen:[30]

> Research shows that weak ties can prove much more helpful in networking, because they form bridges to worlds we do not walk within. Strong ties, on the other hand, tend to be worlds we already know; good friends often know many of the same people and things we know. They are not the best when it comes to searching for new jobs, ideas, experts, and knowledge. Weak ties are also good because … it's less time consuming to talk to someone once a month (weak tie) than twice a week (a strong tie). People can keep up quite a few weak ties without them being a burden.

---

[29] Morten Hansen, *Collaboration: How Leaders Avoid the Traps, Build Common Ground, and Reap Big Results*, Harvard Business Review Press, 2009.

[30] As quoted in Jacob Morgan, "Why Dunbar's Number is Irrelevant," *Social Media Today*, http://socialmediatoday.com/index.php?q=SMC/169132 (Jan. 25, 2010).

Weak Ties or Strong Ties?

So which relationships should I be nurturing—those with my 150 closest friends or with my much larger network of business associates?

I stay connected with everyone in my networks—however strong the tie. I just connect with them in different ways. For weaker ties, I might comment on their blog posts or updates, include them in my newsletter, or join discussions they've started on LinkedIn. For stronger ties, I reach out more regularly—by phone, email, and in person. I invite them to lunch, send them articles or links to websites of interest, offer business tips, introduce them to people they want to meet, or just ask how I can help.

So which relationships should I be nurturing—those with my 150 closest friends or with my much larger network of business associates?

I even stay in touch with "weak" connections in Australia, London, and New Zealand—even though they're half a world away from where I do most of my business. For example, Ivan Levison—an expert copywriter and my neighbor—introduced me to Graham McGregor in New Zealand. Graham was writing a report on "The Unfair Business Advantage" and interviewed me about referral selling. Since then Graham and I speak frequently. He's a master at staying in touch with his referral network. In addition to maintaining a strong Web presence, he sends little books in the mail—packed full of great marketing ideas. We've become friends.

Then there's Will, who wrote to me on LinkedIn, wanting to learn more about referral selling. Will was living in London at the time and has since moved to Australia. We exchanged a few messages and even spoke on the phone. Fast forward two years—I was monitoring a discussion on LinkedIn, during which someone posed a question about converting a sales team to referral selling. My old friend Will wrote a response praising my work. Two days later I received an email from the person who posted the question. He wanted to speak with me about launching referral selling in his company.

Yes, our close connections are always there for us—and probably help us out more than anyone else. But as Hansen points out, there's just not as many of them, and they tend to know many of the same people we know. So stay in touch with those weaker ties as well. You never know when they might be able to provide you with valuable recommendations, referrals, or information, or even just post a few nice words on social media that reach the right person.

In *The Start-Up of You,*[31] LinkedIn's executive chairman and co-founder Reid Hoffman writes, "There's a big difference between being the *most* connected person and being the *best* connected person."

I completely agree. You can waste your time with people who "take, take, take," with no intention of ever giving back. Or you can connect with people who contribute ideas, ask how they can help, and stay in touch. Why do you think LinkedIn doesn't indicate on your profile if you have more than 500 contacts? It's not a race to see who has the most connections. It's the quality of your contacts that matters.

---

[31] Reid Hoffman and Ben Casnocha, *The Start-Up of You: Adapt to the Future, Invest in Yourself, and Transform Your Career,* Crown Business, 2012.

Risky Business

The looming presence and demands of social media present both risks and opportunities for sales. When companies jump into social media without a strategy, they run the risk of not only wasting time—a sales professional's most valuable asset—but also damaging their brands.

With so much information available, you could spend hours a day online—switching back and forth from one social-media site to another—and still not find everything valuable there is to read about a company or prospect. In fact, 81.7 percent of salespeople report feeling challenged by the amount of data available and the time it takes to research a prospect, according to CSO Insights.[32]

Kurt Shaver of the Sales Foundry says that inbound marketing is foreign to many traditional salespeople, who have previously had no responsibility for creating and delivering content—a function that was always handled by their marketing departments. "This is both an opportunity and a risk," says Kurt. "Salespeople are not trained on the company's social-media messaging, and often

---

[32] CSO Insights and Lattice, "2012 Impact of Big Data on Sales Performance: Why Big Data Should be a Big Deal for Sales," 2012.

they're not authorized to publish content on a company's behalf. It's like giving a teenager a car without driving lessons."

What to do?

1. **Assign accountability.** Select a social-media "ambassador" who is in charge of developing your strategy, keeping it on track, and training the sales team on what they should and shouldn't post. Ensure your strategy aligns with your customers' needs and your organization's priorities.

2. **Train your reps.** Teach your sales team how to efficiently and effectively support your company's social-media strategy. This is not about becoming a techno-wizard. It is about maximizing time spent.

Is Social Media Worth Your Time?

First and foremost, if your prospects aren't active on social media, you don't need to show up.

According to Kurt Shaver, there are three industries that really benefit from LinkedIn prospecting:

1. **Information Technology:** IT still ranks as the No. 2 industry, behind Higher Education. With a target-rich environment of more than 10 million members, technology salespeople can benefit tremendously from having a strong LinkedIn network and knowing the ins and outs of how to use the Advanced People Search.

2. **Business Services:** Industries like Commercial Insurance, Commercial Real Estate, and Business Banking benefit from the long-term payoff of a

LinkedIn investment. Unlike the technology business, where salespeople often switch jobs every two to three years, professionals in these industries tend to work in one area for many decades. Success used to be reflected by the size of their Rolodexes and their books of business. Today, savvy professionals can accelerate their success by building long-standing relationships using LinkedIn—"the Rolodex on Steroids."

3. **Marketing and Advertising:** Marketing and Advertising salespeople benefit from the social aspect of LinkedIn news. Spotting trends and reacting quickly is crucial in this fast-paced business. LinkedIn features like Home Page Updates, Individual and Company Follows, and LinkedIn Today provide many ways to stay up-to-date on news that is important to one's own network. Some of the largest LinkedIn Groups are in this industry [including more than half a million members in the eMarketing Association Network].

Of course, salespeople from other industries can benefit from using social media. But before you start spending hours of your precious sales time each week (or each day) online, make sure your clients actually use social media—and are open to connecting with vendors that way.

To use social media effectively, salespeople must learn new skills. They need training on how to utilize the various platforms. But they also must understand how the platforms fit together and how to tailor their communication and behavior for each prospect. Some clients respond best with a LinkedIn message about when to talk, where to meet, and people to contact. Others prefer email or (gulp) an actual phone call. (Different strokes for different folks.)

Don't Get Distracted

Once you've developed your social-media strategy—one that aligns with your company's messaging and takes into account how your clients want to interact with you via social media—the challenge is figuring out how to maximize your social-media efforts without wasting half your day online.

I have personally struggled with how to spend time wisely on social media. I don't want to overlook a promotion or job change for one of my connections (a great excuse to reach out and nurture that relationship). I don't want to risk missing out on a relevant conversation about prospecting and referrals. But I also have a blog to write and my books, articles, and radio show to promote. On the other hand, I don't want to risk starting my day on social media and surfacing at lunch time.

> Before you start spending hours of your precious sales time each week (or each day) online, make sure your clients actually use social media—and are open to connecting with vendors that way.

Thankfully, Barbara Giamanco, president of Social Centered Selling, had the answer for me—a strategy she calls "5 in 15." The goal is to spend 15 minutes each day focused on five specific social-media activities that will get you your desired results (e.g., share a relevant news article, answer a question in a group, write one recommendation, or change out a presentation on your profile).

Get Smart

Obviously, you may spend more than 15 minutes a day on social media, especially if you're using it to conduct research on prospects. But with so much information available, salespeople need new tools to help them harness the power of social intelligence so they can work smarter, not harder.

SECTION 4

WORKING SMARTER: SALES-INTELLIGENCE TOOLS

From a sales perspective, social media means gathering relevant information or, to use the current jargon, "sales intelligence." And boy, is there plenty of information out there!

Conducting research is not only a sales advantage; it's a sales imperative. In her e-book, *9 Things You Need to Know About Social Selling,* Barbara Giamanco explains that while sales remains a relationship-driven business, the power of "who you know" is now trumped by "what you know about who you know." The new social customers are demanding relevance, expecting salespeople to have researched them, their companies, and their needs *before engaging.* This has heightened the need for comprehensive sales intelligence that brings together both traditional data and social media.

Fifty-five percent of B2B survey respondents search for information on social media, according to *Business.com.*[33] And a report from the

---

[33] As cited in Shea Bennett, "How Social is B2B?", *Media Bistro,* http://www.mediabistro.com/alltwitter/b2b-social-marketing_b20019 (March 28, 2012).

Aberdeen Group shows that those who do leverage social intelligence get some pretty impressive results, including:[34]

- Dramatically greater improvement (21.4 percent) in top-line revenue each year, compared to 16.4 percent for all other businesses
- A 9.5-percent annual increase in the number of salespeople who make quota, vs. a 3.4-percent increase for other companies
- A customer-satisfaction rating that improves at nearly twice the rate (5.8 vs. 2.1 percent) of other organizations

Steve Woods—group vice president of software development at Oracle and former chief technology officer for Eloqua—says that social intelligence, when applied effectively, enables salespeople to see events in people's lives and to use that information to make personal connections. "We've never seen this before—the opportunity to deepen a relationship for the relationship's sake, rather than for some specific outcome," he says. "A salesperson with many good, deep, strong relationships will do better." Why? Because social media defines us by our relationships rather than by our facts. "Look at the world of the Rolodex—each individual was a stand-alone island defined by his or her facts. Today, a person exists as an individual at the center of a person's networks. If facts change, that doesn't change who she is at the nexus of her relationships. Those relationships don't disappear."

If you're not using social media to arm yourself with information about

---

[34] Peter Ostrow, "Earned Loyalty: Harnessing Social Media Analytics for Sales Effectiveness," Aberdeen Group, 2012.

your prospects and clients, then you're behind the curve, because you can bet your competitors are doing so (and if not, they will be soon).

Where do you turn for help managing all this information-technology? That's right … more technology. Let's explore some of the robust social-selling tools that help us gather the information we need to wow our prospects.

> Social intelligence, when applied effectively, enables salespeople to see events in people's lives and to use that information to make personal connections.

Mine the Data: Pan for Gold

Customer Relationship Management (CRM), marketing automation, and sales intelligence—they go together like birds of a feather, or jam and bread (hey, there's a song about that). When used wisely, this powerful combination of invaluable sales tools significantly shortens the sales cycle.

It's Not Just CRM Anymore

CRM applications enable us to organize contact information and chart interaction with clients, customers, and prospects. Nearly 80 percent of companies have now implemented CRM systems, according to CSO Insights.[35] But as social media has dramatically increased the amount of "sales intelligence" we're expected to possess, CRM is no longer enough. For the same study, researchers asked salespeople about the effectiveness of their CRM systems at providing internal company information. A whopping 44.3 percent said the systems needed improvement. As for *external* company

[35] CSO Insights and Lattice, "2012 Impact of Big Data on Sales Performance: Why Big Data Should be a Big Deal for Sales," 2012.

information—the most important data for salespeople—only 15.5 percent said their CRM applications met expectations.

Greg Brush, senior vice president of sales for InsideView, believes CRM is a necessary commodity, because it's your foundational database. He explains:

> Think of CRM as the foundation of your house. As you build your house, you have many choices—the floor plan, style, colors, design, etc. The value in your new house is your ability to have a great traffic flow and a place for everything so that you know exactly where to find your car keys when you're dashing out the door. Likewise, the value in CRM is in the information it allows you to document, organize, and quickly access. The time-to-market advantage comes from the effectiveness of the sales team in mining the CRM data and extracting relevant information quickly.

Data, Data Everywhere

Now, here's where my head starts spinning. Yes, I have the tools to access data. But data is not always relevant or interesting, so I must spend time reviewing, assimilating, and assessing whether the information is useful. That's the interpretation part. Then, as a result of my assessment, I might determine I need to get even more data—by reaching out to members of my team, colleagues, clients, or the Internet. I need to verify the accuracy of the data. What is true, and what is urban legend?

> The first responder usually gets the deal—but only if that salesperson also provides accurate and complete information.

Velocity also matters. After all, the first responder usually gets the deal—but only if that salesperson also provides accurate and complete information.

Data access, interpretation, and velocity—it's a delicate balance we must strive for every day. Sometimes we win, and sometimes we get gobbled up.

Your Technology Toolbox

David Satterwhite, vice president of worldwide sales at Appcelerator, says that in addition to sales-force automation, it's important to provide your team with several different database tools for company, customer, and prospect information—such as Hoovers, Jigsaw, or InsideView. He adds, "Tools like Marketo for email marketing are also a must."

Contact Data Isn't Enough

When deciding which databases to use, choose at least one platform that provides more than just contact information. That's where sales-intelligence tools like InsideView, Hoovers, and Data.com come in. These tools scour company websites, social-media pages, and news articles for all the recent, relevant information available on your prospects—and then compile, organize, and deliver all the data to you.

Research suggests that the payoff can be huge. According to a collaborative study from CSO Insights and InsideView, B2B sales win rates were highest when reps used sales-intelligence tools (See Figure 1).

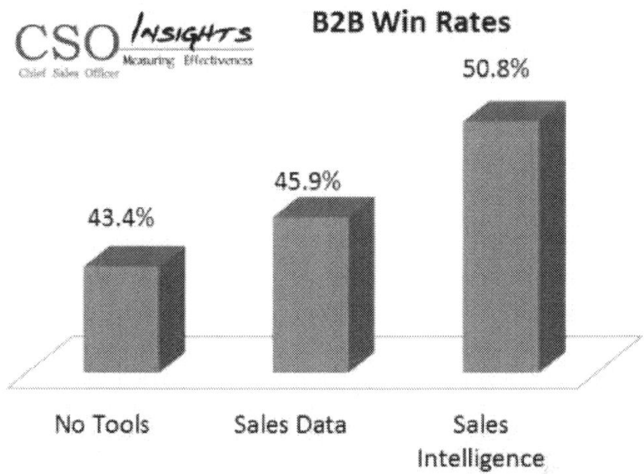

Figure 1: Sales-Intelligence Tools Increased Sales

In addition to helping salespeople increase the number of deals they close, sales-intelligence tools also shorten the time it takes to complete the first few important steps of the sales process—conducting research and finding referral sources through social media. As we know, speed and accuracy win clients.

BUYER 2.0 MEET SELLER 2.0

Buyer 2.0 isn't the only one who has learned to leverage information technology. Seller 2.0 is just as tech savvy—and just as well informed. Today's sales teams are equipped with collaboration tools that help us speed up the sales process, obtain relevant information, connect with colleagues, and talk to real people about the issues of our buyers.

Our prospects might know a lot about us before that initial meeting, but if we're good at what we do, we know just as much (or more) about them. However, as salespeople we are faced with the same challenge as our buyers—there's so much information and so many digital tools that it's hard to know where to put our time (and our money).

Our prospects might know a lot about us before that initial meeting, but if we're good at what we do, we know just as much (or more) about them.

Nancy Nardin, president of Smart Selling Tools, says to ask yourself whether an application provides a net gain in efficiency. "Good tools increase our productivity," says Nancy, "*without* requiring us to change habits or workflows, and without introducing new barriers."

For instance, she says, CRM is not an efficiency tool. "Most CRM systems are too cumbersome. In some ways, they save time, but they also introduce a new *consumption* of time. Someone has to populate and manage the tools. CRM is useful, but it doesn't add productivity."

While CRM is probably worth the time, there are plenty of other tools that aren't. So which tools *are* valuable? Here are a few recommendations from Nancy:

Know When Your Buyer Is Ready

Applications like ToutApp and Yesware alert you anytime a buyer engages with an email from you—even if you sent it months ago. Let's say you speak to a prospect and agree it's not the right time to work together. Then three months from now, she opens an old email from you. Maybe she's reviewing the budgets or was simply thinking about touching base with you. Either way, you know it's a good time to call and check in.

Conversation Tips

Applications like ShadeTree Technology, Revegy, and Qvidian are great for conducting research and learning what to say on that initial call. They provide insight on what is relevant to our prospects—the issues they care about right now.

Collaboration Tools

Salesforce.com's Chatter and LinkedIn's Sales Navigator are productivity tools that help salespeople access inside information in a nanosecond (almost). You can monitor the people, groups, and projects that matter most to you in one spot. With real-time feeds, your teams can work together on fast-moving issues, such as sales pursuits, customer projects, and marketing campaigns. You can also work with external customers, vendors, and partners—with 100-percent control over what they can access.

InsideView's Private Connection Cloud enables you to sync your personal social networks to your corporate-connection network—creating a powerful, private asset that you and your team can leverage. This way, you can easily identify important relationships with prospects and get referrals through your previous employers, reference accounts, personal connections, and education details.

LinkedIn, and Twitter, and Facebook ... It Never Stops

Social-media-management programs like HootSuite, TwitterFeed, Ping.fm, and TweetDeck are invaluable tools for your technology arsenal. If you've got an article to post, an announcement to make, or information you want to share, you don't have to log onto your blog as well as your LinkedIn, Facebook, and Twitter accounts. Instead, you can update them all from a single dashboard, schedule messages to reach your contacts or followers when they're most likely to be online, and get metrics for the traffic on your profile pages.

There are lots of great tech tools—including these and many more. But not every tool is right for every salesperson. So find what works best for you. Just remember, if it's not saving you time and making your job easier, it's *wasting* your time.

BEYOND SOCIAL INTELLIGENCE

You can arm yourself with all the social intelligence available on a prospect, but it isn't likely to give you an advantage over your competitors, who have probably done their research too. Clients now *expect* you to know all about their companies.

What *will* set you apart from the rest and get you in front of decision-makers hasn't changed a bit; it's still a personal connection and a referral from someone the client trusts.

Miles Austin, otherwise known as "The Web Tools Guy," writes the following in his blog post, "Social Selling Is Not for the Lazy":[36]

> I attribute one of my favorite quotes about Web tools to Trish Bertuzzi, president of The Bridge Group: **"A fool with a tool is still a fool."**
>
> Now that is from a gal who has and is leading a sales organization that is successful in this new economy. She knows full well the hard work that is still required to achieve success in sales.

---

[36]Miles Austin, "Social Selling is Not for the Lazy," *Fill the Funnel*, http://www.fillthefunnel.com/social-selling-is-not-for-the-lazy/.

> Social selling is a great way to expedite the first few important steps in prospecting—researching potential clients and identifying referral sources. Beyond that, it's not social intelligence we need; it's *relationship* intelligence that seals the deal.

To this, Miles adds: **"A fool using Social Selling is still broke."**

Trish and Miles got it right. In fact, I'll add my own iteration: **"A fool with social-selling tools who doesn't have a referral is still broke."**

Since referral prospecting is, and always will be, the way I work, I have integrated social selling into my process. First, I speak with clients and colleagues to identify companies that could be great clients for me. I follow these companies on social media and research them with sales-intelligence tools. Next, I search my LinkedIn contacts to determine where I have the strongest connections. From there, my sales process is the same as it always has been. I reach out to my strongest referral sources and ask for referral introductions.

Social selling is a great way to expedite the first few important steps in prospecting—researching potential clients and identifying referral sources. Beyond that, it's not social intelligence we need; it's *relationship* intelligence that seals the deal.

The problem is that we get so enamored with—and addicted to—technology, and we sometimes let it take over our lives and our sales processes. Winning in Sales 2.0 means leveraging technology and also learning how to keep it in its place.

SECTION 5

KEEP TECHNOLOGY IN ITS PLACE

These are exciting times. We have more information at our fingertips than any of us could have imagined—even just 10 years ago. The ease and speed with which we communicate with people all over the world creates an increasingly-global society and marketplace. The tech world changes so quickly that one can only wonder what science-fiction-like technology will become a reality over the next decade.

Technology makes our lives (and work) more exciting and, in many ways, more efficient. But for many of us, it has also wreaked havoc on our relationships and ability to function in the real world. With mounds of information and data bombarding us, and management on our backs to do more with less, how do we choose the right course with so many competing priorities?

> When it comes to balance, technology is a double-edged sword.

When it comes to balance, technology is a double-edged sword. On the one hand, it enables us to dictate our own schedules and to work when it is most convenient. But our dependence on technology can also get out of hand, and before we know it, the technology that was supposed to make our lives easier is suddenly running our lives. We can't sleep without our smart phones within reaching distance. Even on vacation, we bring work with us (or at the very least, clients can reach us). We can't even get through a conversation with a client or prospect without showing off some sort of tech savvy.

We often forget that technology is only a tool and that our greatest asset is—and always will be—ourselves.

TECHNOLOGY LAGGARDS

Are you a digital native or a digital immigrant?

When I asked one colleague this question, she said she was "still on the boat." Her comment reminded me of my Aunt Gert, to whom my first book was dedicated. She lived to be 93 years old, and when she was in her late 80s, we wanted to show her how to use a computer. Not only was she completely disinterested, but she told us that she still didn't know how the radio worked, so we should forget it.

On the other hand, my aunt Leona could be considered somewhat of a digital native, even though she was born in 1916. She was the first person I knew who had a computer. I remember when she showed us the Prodigy program and all it could do. She was ecstatic about the time it saved her and how it organized all of her records. This was the late '80s. We stood there rather disinterested, thinking this was probably another of her passing phases. You see, Aunt Leona was always way ahead of the game.

When the Northridge earthquake hit the Los Angeles area on January 17, 1994, Aunt Leona's building was condemned, and she and Uncle Joel had to move. The first thing Leona said was: "I have to get my computer. Everything's on it." Until her early 90s, she was still writing and sending emails and maintaining electronic files.

Unlike Aunt Leona, you're probably somewhere in between a digital immigrant and digital native. Some of us view technology as intrusive, overwhelming, and a source of unnecessary complexity. Others depend entirely on technology to run their businesses and lives.

Recently I was late for a client call, and I was mortified. I'm always (mostly) on time. My excuse? My computer didn't beep. I was busy working on a project and lost track of time, and Outlook didn't remind me to make the call.

Yes, I wear a watch. Yes, I can see the time on my computer. But I became so dependent on technology that I got careless and lazy. I guarantee that won't happen again.

Confession: I use a paper calendar. My children are amused by this, but I can find appointments twice as fast as they can by quickly opening to a page in my agenda. They're still booting up their electronic calendars, and I'm tapping my fingers at the delay. I'm not a total Luddite. I also use an electronic calendar—mainly because that's how my clients work. Unless I send a meeting request and the person accepts, the meeting won't happen. That time is blocked, and no one can postpone without the consent of the originator. It's efficient and makes sense.

I don't scan QR codes on business cards (although I might have changed my behavior by the time you read this). I like to look at people's cards, to feel the paper and then look them in the eyes and comment on their cards. There's something very personal about that interaction.

I guess you could say I'm a digital immigrant. I certainly wasn't born into a technology-powered world, nor did I instinctively adapt to it the way Aunt Leona did. But for the most part, I have assimilated. I still maintain some of the "old-fashioned" ways of doing things, but recognizing the value and importance of technology in today's business world, I have embraced and adopted most modern technologies—especially those that are imperative for success in Sales 2.0.

Dawn Westerberg of Dawn Westerberg Consulting believes that many of us are lagging behind when it comes to recognizing the way technology changes how we sell and market. "Many business owners curl into a fetal position and coast on their customer base until retirement," says Dawn. "They say, 'Don't make me learn new technologies.' They dismiss social media and blogging. They continue to pay someone to call their lists of thousands, even though it's not working for them."

Message for those still on the boat: It's time to disembark. The world has changed and so has the sales game. If you're not using technology to grow your business, you're not playing on a level field with your competitors.

If you're not using technology to grow your business, you're not playing on a level field with your competitors.

That being said, if you're not a digital native, that's OK. In fact, as digital immigrants, we have the advantage of understanding both the value *and the limitations* of technology.

Ditch the Demo

Why is "I'd love to give you a demo" one of the first things we hear from a software salesperson? Of course you would. You want to show me your cool technology with all the bells and whistles. That's the easy part, and many people mistakenly think it's the impressive part. Not true.

The best demo is no demo. Solid, smart salespeople focus on their clients' pain points. As a buyer, I don't care a flip about how your technology works until I know what it can do for *my business.* The same is true for your prospects and clients.

As a buyer, I don't care a flip about how your technology works until I know what it can do for *my business.* The same is true for your prospects and clients.

Sound harsh? You bet. But the truth is that we easily slip into our corporate or tech jargon and forget that we're not here to push product. We're here to connect the dots between a client's problem and our solution. This is especially true today, because thanks to the Internet, your prospects have probably read up on your product before they ever agreed to meet with you. Heck, they probably watched that same demo on your website.

And the more high-level your prospects are, the less they care how your software works or what the new tools look like. They just care about the end result.

Understanding this dynamic, a sales VP I know challenged her team to leave the sales engineers (and their demos) at the office for introductory sales calls. She explained that their goal was to ask questions and uncover the prospects' pain. Period. And to that I say, "Bravo!"

Clients don't need your tutorial. They need *you.*

Forget the demo, or at the very least, don't lead with it. Start by listening, asking questions, and learning more about your prospects' business challenges. It's hard work, but if we leave the work to our clients, we won't get the sale.

One Throat to Choke

As a buyer, one of the most valuable aspects of having a relationship with a salesperson (versus buying online) is accountability—having a point of contact within the company, one person to give the credit (and commission) and one throat to choke when something goes wrong.

> When customers have exhausted online options to get more services or resolve a problem, they want to talk to a real person ... *now*!

Electronic phone trees are the bane of customer service. Full disclosure: I've yelled at the phone while on hold—seemingly forever. I get especially frustrated when a calm, recorded voice tells me the company values my business. If they really valued my business, they'd pick up the phone—not pass me from one list of automated options to another, or from one person to another, each guessing at who might have the answer to my question. And then they have the audacity to ask me to spend even more time completing a survey. I know they don't do anything with those surveys, and I'm not going to bother. It's a waste of my time. (I'm getting frustrated just *writing* about it!)

When customers have exhausted online options to get more services or resolve a problem, they want to talk to a real person ... *now*! The more layers of technology they have to navigate, the more frustrated they are by the time they get on the phone with you. There's always a point when a customer needs to make contact. That's when you must show up, ask the right questions, and deliver answers.

Technology Addiction—Yes, There Really Is Such a Thing

I'm addicted to sugar—especially dark chocolate. I know that about myself and am prepared to deal with the consequences. But my vice doesn't prevent me from building relationships and enjoying other people's company. A technology addiction, on the other hand, does.

At a recent conference, another attendee sat at my table and proceeded to pull an iPhone, iPod, *and* laptop from her bag. She placed each device on the table and worked on all three of them during the entire presentation. Maybe she was tweeting, answering emails, or writing a blog post. I'll never know for sure. But I do know she couldn't possibly have given her full attention to the speaker. So much for being present.

As I watched her peck away at one keyboard after another, I couldn't help but wonder why she bothered to attend in the first place. How could she possibly connect with the speakers, her fellow tablemates, and other conference attendees when she couldn't take her eyes off her gadgets? Isn't that the whole point of such networking events—to talk to real, live people?

Do You Need an Intervention?

Not only is technology addiction a real thing; it's becoming a widespread pandemic.

I was amazed when I learned that technology addiction is a real condition. I first read about it in a *San Francisco Chronicle* article entitled "Internet Addiction Can Harm Real Relationships,"[37] which explains:

> Technology can be seductive because it provides an instant reward—a text message from a friend, success in a video game or stimulating news on a Web site—that is not necessarily harmful.
>
> But mental health experts say an addiction can form—just as with gambling—when people keep seeking that intermittent, unpredictable reward.
>
> "The fact that it is unpredictable is what compels the brain to keep checking over and over and over," said Dr. David Greenfield, assistant clinical professor of psychiatry at the University of Connecticut School of Medicine. "When people are afraid of not having their … phone[s] with them, then it's addictive."

Not only is technology addiction a real thing; it's becoming a widespread pandemic.

---

[37] Benny Evangelista, "Internet addiction can harm real relationships," *SFGate*, http://www.sfgate.com/business/article/Internet-addiction-can-harm-real-relationships-3281034.php (Nov. 15, 2009).

In "Is Technology the New Opiate of the Masses?,"[38] psychologist Jim Taylor cites two recent studies on the topic. One found that 61 percent of Americans say they are addicted to the Internet. The other reported that "addicted" is the word most people use to describe their relationship to technology.

Stop Texting and Start Connecting

The next time you're out in public, take a look around you. Notice all the people on their mobile phones. When you walk down the street, pay attention to how many people are talking on their cells, texting, or surfing the Web as they walk—or worse, while they are driving.

Casey Neistat, a New York-based filmmaker, shares the following perspective (as well as a brilliant video about the rules of "Texting While Walking"[39]) in *The New York Times* Opinion Pages: "Navigating the sidewalks of New York City can be as challenging as any rushing sport, like football or rugby. But when your opponents are walking while text messaging, their field of view is impaired, and this can render a three-block walk to Starbucks somewhere between infuriating and life-threatening."

When we zero in on the technology in front of us, we stop paying attention to the people around us. We forget about things like common courtesy and respecting others.

---

[38] Jim Taylor, Ph.D., "Is technology the new opiate of the masses?," *SFGate*, http://blog.sfgate.com/jtaylor/2012/04/26/is-technology-the-new-opiate-of-the-masses/ (April 26).

[39] Casey Neistat, "Texting While Walking," http://www.youtube.com/watch?v=pLA1UelcDrE (Jan. 19, 2012).

As Eric Schmidt, executive chairman of Google, told the 2012 graduating class of Boston University: "Take one hour a day and turn that thing off ... Take your eyes off that screen and look into the eyes of the person you love. Have a conversation, a real conversation."

Technology connects us to the outside world, but what about connecting to the world right in front of us?

YOUR REAL LIFE IS RIGHT IN FRONT OF YOU

What happened to actually paying attention to the person in front of you—the person with whom you arranged to spend time?

On any given weekend morning, you can observe couples and friends out at restaurants eating brunch. I used to be amazed at how people could share a meal, enjoy their first cup of coffee, and read the newspaper—all without saying a word to each other. Why bother going out? Some people say it's a sign of an established relationship when you don't have to speak to be together. I don't buy it.

Now it's even worse. People no longer bring newspapers; they bring their smart phones. I recently observed this behavior when my husband and I went out for brunch. For at least 15 minutes, the couple next to us sat in silence, tapping away on their phones and never exchanging a word.

What happened to actually paying attention to the person in front of you—the person with whom you arranged to spend time?

Sherry Turkle—a psychologist, MIT professor, and author of *Alone Together: Why We Expect More From Technology and Less From Each Other*[40]—writes about this sad phenomenon in her *New York Times* article, "The Flight from Conversation":

> We live in a technological universe in which we are always communicating. And yet we have sacrificed conversation for mere connection.
>
> At home, families sit together, texting and reading email. At work, executives text during board meetings. We text (and shop and go on Facebook) during classes and when we're on dates. My students tell me about an important new skill: it involves maintaining eye contact with someone while you text someone else; it's hard, but it can be done.
>
> Over the past 15 years, I've studied technologies of mobile connection and talked to hundreds of people of all ages and circumstances about their plugged-in lives. I've learned that the little devices most of us carry around are so powerful that they change not only what we do, but also who we are.
>
> We've become accustomed to a new way of being "alone together."

---

[40] Sherry Turkle, *Alone Together: Why We Expect More from Technology and Less from Each Other*, Basic Books, 2012.

Bring Back Balance

Has our dependence on technology gone a little too far? And is it slowly taking away our ability to talk to each other?

New, fancy technology is alluring. It's easy to get sucked into the digital universe. But our relationships are what really matter—in life and business. This is true for everyone, but even more so for salespeople, whose *job* is to build relationships. We cannot lose (or set aside) our ability to connect person-to-person, not if we ever intend to expand our networks and close deals.

> It's easy to get sucked into the digital universe. But our relationships are what really matter—in life and business.

When we're constantly checking our phones to make sure we're not missing something "out there," we're missing out on opportunities to connect with the people right in front of us. In average conversations, adults make eye contact between 30 and 60 percent of the time, according to communications-analytics company Quantified Impressions.[41] But the same study shows that people should be making eye contact 60 to 70 percent of the time to create a sense of emotional connection.

The last thing smart salespeople want to do is weaken the relationships we have worked so hard to build. Technology

---

[41] *Quantified Impressions*, "Eye Contact – A Declining Communications Tool?", http://www.quantifiedimpressions.com/blog/eye-contact-a-declining-communications-tool/ (June 27).

provides valuable tools for advertising, marketing, and sales research. But actually closing deals is about connecting, one human being to another, listening and providing tailored solutions to clients' unique problems. If we stop doing that, technology will have done what I said in the beginning of this book that it cannot do—replace salespeople.

People do business with people. Period. So put down the toys and talk to people. Or better yet, meet in person. It takes more time, but I guarantee your results will prove the time was well spent.

Are You Addicted to Technology?

Here are some questions to consider if you think you might be addicted to the Internet:[42]

- Do you spend excessive time online, or more than you intended?
- Do you feel more depressed or lonely the more time you spend online?
- Do you have a heightened sense of euphoria while online or using a computer?
- Is it interfering with your job or school performance?
- Do family or friends complain about the time and energy you spend online?

---

[42] Excerpted from Benny Evangelista, "Internet Addiction Can Harm Real Relationships," *SFGate*, http://www.sfgate.com/business/article/Internet-addiction-can-harm-real-relationships-3281034.php (Nov. 15, 2009).

- Do you frequently choose spending time online over going out with other people?
- Do you hide, lie or become defensive about online activities?
- Do you feel depressed, restless, moody or nervous offline and fine again when online?
- Do you spend too much time with online pornography, multiplayer games or gambling sites?

If you are addicted, fear not. You just need a little rehabilitation. Here are a few steps in the right direction:

- Unplug yourself completely from technology for at least a few moments each day.
- Keep track of how much you use technology, and moderate overuse.
- If needed, seek counseling, self-help or support groups.

Is Your Smart Phone Making You Socially Dumb?

For most busy professionals, smart phones are a "must have." But over-dependency on them can ruin relationships—both business and personal. That's why Joey Reiman, founder and CEO of BrightHouse and author of *Thinking for a Living,*[43] created the

---

[43] Joey Reiman. *Thinking for a Living: Creating Ideas that Revitalize Your Business, Career, and Life,* Taylor Trade Publishing, 2001.

Blackberry 10 Commandments[44]—rules to live by whether you have a Blackberry, iPhone, Android, or some other device not yet invented:

1. Thou shalt not take the BlackBerry to any table with food on it or family around it. A BlackBerry is not a fruit, nor does it come from a tree.

2. Thou shalt not use the BlackBerry as reading material in the event of insomnia. It will only worsen your situation.

3. Though shalt not BlackBerry in lieu of responding to a child's request (e.g., "Wait a second. I'm reading something.")

4. Thou shalt not place the BlackBerry within distance of hearing its incessant beeps while at home. It is not a bird.

5. Thou shalt not check the BlackBerry as if it were your baby. It will not cry or stop breathing.

6. Thou shalt not confuse the number of emails with self-worth.

7. Thou shalt do everything possible to misplace your BlackBerry on weekends. "There's No Place Like Home" will never be the tagline for the BlackBerry company.

8. Thou shalt remember that a BlackBerry is not a body appendage. It is a device that belongs in your briefcase, on your desk and not in social settings.

---

[44] Reprinted with permission from *PINK magazine (littlepinkbook.com).*

9. Thou shalt refrain from bringing the BlackBerry to events involving family interaction. Extraneous dialogue with this contraption in lieu of real conversation suggests addiction.

10. Thou shalt never, ever, ever bring the BlackBerry to bed. Do this and you are BlackBuried.

SECTION 6

MARKETING MATTERS

Technology might not have changed *how* we sell, but it's certainly changed how we market. With new, sophisticated Web applications, social media, the cloud, and the skyrocketing adoption of mobility, marketers and advertisers alike have been scrambling to figure out how rapidly-changing technologies impact the way we reach customers and craft our messaging.

Brian Solis, author of *The End of Business as Usual*,[45] says that reaching customers today is not about modifying what we're doing; it's a total transformation. Here are a few excerpts from his blog about the "The New Multiscreen World":[46]

> How you design, sell, market, and serve will require nothing short of complete transformation over the

---

[45] Brian Solis, *The End of Business as Usual: Rewire the Way You Work to Succeed in the Consumer Revolution*, Wiley, 2011.

[46] Brian Solis, "We are now a society of multi-taskers and multi-screeners," http://www.briansolis.com/2012/12/we-are-now-a-society-of-multi-taskers-and-multi-screeners/ (Dec. 18, 2012).

> next 10 years. This is true in not only how you engage connected customers but employees as well. It's a lifestyle and as businesses, we must become connected to earn relevance. If we don't, then we earn just the opposite, irrelevance. I refer to this transitory economic state as Digital Darwinism, when technology and society evolve faster than the ability to adapt.
>
> Not only are consumers spending a significant amount of time on multiple devices outside of work, they're doing so at the same time.
>
> TV—43 minutes
>
> PC/Laptop—39
>
> Tablet—30
>
> Smartphone—17
>
> In short, your customer base is fragmented. Just showing up in new channels and creating website-like presences in social networks isn't enough. Designing apps or creating digital assets for mobile devices is only part of the solution. Without a vision, an articulation of the overall experience and how customer engagement takes shape in each channel and as a whole, any work you do may hurt more than it helps.

What does this mean for salespeople? How do we get close to customers when their attention is so fragmented? If we want to reach our multi-tasking, multi-device-using buyers, then improving communication between marketing and sales is critical. Our buyers are everywhere, so we must communicate with them across media channels.

For generations, sales and marketing departments have been at odds in most companies, but none of us has time for sibling rivalry today. Our marketing teams can be more valuable to us than ever before. While they figure out how to best utilize the technologies that enable us to stay in touch with clients, we should be doing what we do best—building relationships with customers, getting referrals, and closing deals.

For generations, sales and marketing departments have been at odds in most companies, but none of us has time for sibling rivalry today.

DRIP, DRIP, DRIP

The move from direct to digital marketing, and from event to nurture—or "drip"—marketing, requires a rapid adoption of technology. With this shift, direct-mail budgets decrease, while digital-marketing budgets increase—for email, webcasts, and marketing automation.

Dan Druker, chief marketing officer at MyBuys, adds:

> Marketing is no longer just one campaign to the next; it's about the whole life-cycle of the buyer—name, suspect, prospect, and opportunity. Nurture marketing allows us to develop customized communications for every step in that process. This is the No. 1 change in marketing, and it is enabled through technology.

Nurture marketing makes sense, because it offers a low-cost way to do what great salespeople have always done—provide information and value to our customers.

Dan is such a big proponent of nurture marketing that, when he was senior vice president of marketing for Intaact Corporation, he dedicated an entire team to it. This team was in charge of getting prospects to where they were ready to begin the sales process. Meanwhile salespeople only worked on active deals. They were exclusively devoted to closing, while the nurturing team was responsible for all interaction with prospects up until and after the point of sale. When a salesperson got a referral, and the prospect wasn't ready to buy, the lead went straight to the nurturing team.

Nurture Marketing Doesn't Get You Off the Hook for Relationship Building

I'm a big fan of Dan's, but here's where our opinions differ. I am a firm believer that salespeople should start building relationships with prospects as soon as possible—and that we should maintain those relationships during and after the sale.

When I asked Dan what would happen if his sales reps had leveraged every one of their customer relationships to get introductions to new clients, he said this would take away from the time they should be closing and that this strategy doesn't scale.

Yet, he agrees that referrals have the highest rate of conversion, the highest close rate, and the lowest cost of any business-development strategy. He says referred prospects have conversion rates of 80 percent from lead to opportunity and 60 percent from opportunity to close, performing two to three times as well as other lead sources.

> It's up to salespeople to nurture their own relationships—not just with marketing automation, but with one-on-one conversations.

My point exactly: Referrals are, hands down, the best way to generate qualified leads. And how do we get referrals? We keep building our referral networks.

Nurture marketing only takes us so far. It's up to salespeople to nurture their own relationships—not just with marketing automation, but with one-on-one conversations.

Rich Dorfman, partner and vice president of client and professional services for Convergent Computing, echoes these sentiments. He says that while CRM and marketing automation are great ways to organize information and to communicate, this technology can also provide us with data that is misleading, incorrect, or incomplete. For example, it cannot tell us what's blocking us from closing deals with certain prospects, because the richness of conversations between reps and prospects are not tracked.

As Rich explains:

> Much of what we learn about our prospects never makes it into the computer. It's in our heads. And salespeople don't want to take the time to document. What makes them good salespeople makes them bad data-entry people. So we may list opportunities, and marketing can help us roll that up in technology. But it doesn't help as much as a five-minute conversation about what needs to happen and who are the players.

While marketing automation is a great tool in our relationship-building toolboxes, it can't be the only contact we have with our clients. Truly nurturing relationships is about more than marketing. It's about talking to people and spending time with them.

Should Salespeople Generate Their Own Leads?

When I began spreading the message about referral selling, I did not, I admit, have a very high opinion of marketing. I didn't have great experiences with marketing departments when I worked in the corporate world. Marketing wrote a bunch of stuff and threw it over the wall for sales to use. They never talked to us, and I re-wrote practically everything.

I recall a time when they devised a unique product promotion. They sent our prospects—who were VPs of sales—a video with information about our new product. Salespeople were tasked with following up and scheduling conversations. And, of course, the marketing department provided a script.

You can probably imagine where that went—nowhere. There I was, sitting in my office, cold calling VPs who had no desire to get on the phone with me. It was a total waste of my time, and that strategy was the opposite of how we were taught to sell.

Therefore, I arrived jaded when I attended my first marketing conference last year. I listened to one marketing professional after another state how great they were at qualifying leads for sales. I learned about MQLs and SQLs and SLAs. Alas, many were frustrated that sales didn't accept a lot of their leads.

During the break, I met a marketing person from one of my client companies. I asked if she knew my client, the SVP of worldwide sales. Her answer: "We don't interact with sales much."

I tried not to show my shock and disbelief, but I'm not sure I was successful. After all, what is the point of marketing if not to support sales? And how can you possibly do that if the two departments don't interact?

Overall, I learned a lot and left that conference thinking I should attend another. At the very least, I might hear someone say something I disagreed with—which could provide interesting material for my blog.

What is the point of marketing if not to support sales? And how can you possibly do that if the two departments don't interact?

At the next conference, I co-presented with a marketing expert who left me flabbergasted when he said, "Salespeople should not generate their own leads. That's the job of marketing." He even had the nerve to add: "And salespeople are terrible at it."

Once I picked my jaw up off the floor, I realized I had attended one marketing conference too many.

Hey, That's My Job!

Don't get me wrong. Our marketing teams provide invaluable support. They bring prospects to our websites, nurture relationships, conduct research, create demographics, write case studies, and build social-media strategies. I have worked with and learned from some great marketers, and I have seen well-aligned sales and marketing teams produce significant results. But one thing marketing should not be doing is qualifying leads. That's our job.

Sales and marketing have complementary roles. We shouldn't be doing each other's jobs.

When marketing routes people to our websites for information or to view a demo, these people are not yet qualified. They're inquiries, people collecting research, "tire kickers," or those just interested in free stuff. Or worse, they're our competitors engaging in a little espionage. None of these are leads.

Ken Krogue, president of InsideSales.com, advocates for striking a balance between warm calling and inbound marketing. He says that while many B2B companies stand to benefit from an expanded inbound marketing presence, it's not enough to score those big-name accounts.

Although Ken's company uses inbound marketing extensively, it doesn't generate the large-scale leads he needs in order to sell to major players like the Fortune 500. "If you look at a typical bell curve, 70 percent of all inbound leads that come in are small," he explains. "To score deals with enterprise-class companies, we have to reach out and initiate conversations, and *then* move to a Web-based type of nurturing."

Sales and marketing have complementary roles. We shouldn't be doing each other's jobs.

Sales, and only sales, can truly determine if a lead is qualified. Why? Because we're responsible for business development, client relationships, and making quota. Not to mention the fact that we're better at it. After all, it's what we do every single day.

Not only is generating leads your responsibility, it's a task you don't want marketing (or anyone else) doing for you. These are your clients, and hopefully you're going to be working with them for a long time. These are also the people who can send you the best, hottest referrals, so you want them to be the right fit for you.

You Call That a Lead?

It's time to change how we talk about sales leads. Inquiries are not leads, and neither are those "coveted" lists of names. Suggesting otherwise borders on insulting.

Leads are people who express interest in discussing your product or service. They match the profile of your ideal client. They have budget—and a need. And they *want* to learn more about how you can help grow their businesses.

I'm not just splitting hairs over terminology. It is downright misrepresentation when companies position themselves as lead-generation experts. It sounds so good (so easy), and so we jump. That's how we get our sales funnels clogged with cold leads that waste our time and almost never pan out.

Good salespeople know how to build qualified pipelines. That's our job, and we're good at it. Marketing has its own role to play—an important, critical one. We need their help more today than ever ... just not with qualifying leads.

The Sales vs. Marketing Showdown: A Salesperson's Perspective

In our fast-paced, tech-driven business climate, no one has time for in-house bickering and tugs-of-war. The battle between sales and marketing has been raging since … well, probably since the advent of marketing. But it's time to call a cease fire.

After all, as much as marketing might bug us, we need their expertise to stay top of mind for our prospects and clients—to create case studies, webinars, events, and other outreach strategies. We need their creativity to build and implement our sales plans—and to help us figure out the best way to leverage social media.

In order to get sales and marketing to play nicely together, we must first understand the root cause of all the animosity. In "Why Sales Hates Marketing,"[47] a 2012 blog from *Inc.com*, author Geoffrey James lists the nine most common complaints he hears from

[47] Geoffrey James, "Why Sales Hates Marketing: 9 Reasons," *Inc.*, http://www.inc.com/geoffrey-james/why-sales-hates-marketing-9-reasons.html (Jan. 24, 2012).

In order to get sales and marketing to play nicely together, we must first understand the root cause of all the animosity.

salespeople about their marketing counterparts—as well as some insightful advice on how to mend those burned bridges.

Below is an excerpt:[48]

1. *Marketing Acts Superior*

Many marketers have business degrees, so they think they're better than sales reps who don't. However, business degrees are of limited use in sales situations—because very few business schools offer courses in sales, let alone majors or degrees.

Since what's taught in b-school is (frankly) a mix of accounting and biz-blab, the superior air of the MBAs is neither appropriate nor helpful.

The Fix: Make certain that every marketer you hire has at least six months of experience selling something.

2. *Marketing Doesn't Believe in Sales*

Marketers are often taught in b-school that good marketing makes a sales force unnecessary. As Peter Drucker put it: "The aim of marketing is to make

[48] Reprinted with permission from the author, Geoffrey James.

selling superfluous" and "the right motto for business management should increasingly be 'from selling to marketing.'"

However, unless a product is a plug-and-play commodity, your only differentiator is how you sell it.

The Fix: Make it clear in the charter of the marketing team that they are there to support the sales team, not to replace it.

3. *Marketing Thinks Selling Is Easy*

Marketers think that they can create so much demand that selling consists of taking orders. However, many "demand creation" activities don't create all that much demand—especially in B2B, where customers generally ignore ads, brochures, and such. And, of course, anyone who's ever sold knows exactly how difficult it can be.

The Fix: Have the marketers make sales calls—or field inside sales calls—so they can see how hard it is.

4. *Marketing Avoids Being Measured*

Marketers generally get paid when they produce leads, brochures, white papers, and so forth—even if none of that activity results in a single sale. They successfully get themselves measured on the deliverables, rather than whether the deliverables have a measurable financial impact.

The Fix: Compensate marketers on the ability of the current sales team to generate revenue and profit from the sales leads that marketing produces. *(Note from Joanne: In many companies, marketing departments are now being measured on the qualified leads they send to sales and the leads that salespeople accept. My guess—and hope—is that as sales and marketing begin to collaborate on client deals, they will have goals and incentives around revenue generation as well.)*

5. *Marketing Claims to be 'Driving Sales'*

Ugh. I've heard this phrase dozens of time from marketers who are trying to take credit for sales, even when they had absolutely no impact on making those sales take place. It's a perfect example of the "law of inverse relevancy," which is "the more you don't plan on doing something, the more you must talk about it."

The Fix: Make Marketing subservient to Sales on the organization chart.

6. *Marketing Pretends It's Strategic*

Give me a break. Brand is a reflection of product and service. If those are good, the brand is good; if not, the brand is bad. Yeah, branding activities help—but the idea that marketers are "brand managers" who should be directing all activities throughout the company is, frankly, ridiculous.

The Fix: Reward marketers for behavior that directly results in a measurable increase in revenue and profit.

7. Marketing Wastes Money

Needless to say, Sales is perfectly capable of wasting money (big time). However, there's also no question that marketers often expend cash on fancy brochures, advertisements, and trade show junkets that have little or no business value. And, let's face it, the more that's spent on marketing boondoggles, the less money there is for commissions.

The Fix: Give the sales team veto power over all pricey marketing activities.

> What the marketers fail to realize is that a lead is only good if it's possible (or even easy) for the sales team to close. Otherwise, it's a waste of time.

8. Marketing Pretends It's Engineering

Once again, give me a break. While marketers often attempt to set a firm's technical direction, most of the time, the marketers have never even spoken to a customer—and have no idea what's technically feasible.

The Fix: Let your engineers do the engineering. That's what you pay them for.

9. *Marketing Argues About Lead Quality*

Marketing frequently provides Sales with lists of unqualified or under-qualified leads, and then accuses Sales of being clueless because it can't close the deals. What the marketers fail to realize is that a lead is only good if it's possible (or even easy) for the sales team to close. Otherwise, it's a waste of time.

The Fix: Reassign (or fire) marketers who can't provide leads that the sales team can close.

The Sales vs. Marketing Showdown: A Marketer's Perspective

While reading the previous comments from Geoffrey James, I bet you were nodding your head, feeling vindicated by the assertion that marketing is to blame for the animosity between our two departments. Being a salesperson myself, I tend to agree with most of Geoffrey's points. But as we all know, there are two sides to every story, and the truth usually lies somewhere in between.

As much as you might love or hate marketing, it's an important part of the sales team, and when we collaborate on both a strategic and tactical basis, we can do great things together.

Christine Crandell is the president of New Business Strategies and a regular contributor to Forbes.com, where she writes about the issues B2B sales and marketing leaders face. She says:

> There is a myth about misalignment—that it only hurts sales. Misalignment hurts the whole company. It lowers revenue, drives up expenses, hurts customer relationships, and can turn the company culture into a toxic situation. It's a multibillion-dollar problem—all because two people, the chief marketing officer and the head of sales, can't get along.

It's Time to Play Nice

There is a myth about misalignment—that it only hurts sales. Misalignment hurts the whole company.

What happens when these departments learn to work together? Everybody wins.

In her blog, "How Alignment Helped Sales Win,"[49] Christine shares the following example:

> This very large B2B enterprise technology vendor had an equally large retailer as a target account they wanted to win. The sales team did all the usual stuff—cold calling, networking, sending letters, and inviting executive management to events. But all that effort wasn't breaking through the noise. Sales came to Marketing and asked for help, not expecting much.
>
> The actual response Sales got was completely different. Marketing wanted to ride along on sales calls, to better understand what they were facing. They wanted to review past interactions and dig deep into the account plan. Then Marketing went off and researched the target account by talking to Wall Street industry analysts, suppliers, front-line employees, and reporters. What they learned was the retailer's values, culture,

---

[49] Christine Crandell, "How Alignment Helped Sales Win," *Forbes*, http://www.forbes.com/sites/christinecrandell/2011/08/14/how-alignment-helped-sales-win/ (Aug. 14, 2011).

work habits and, more importantly, the interests and travel habits of the retailer's executive management. Armed with that information, Marketing embarked on a campaign of "be where they go," which included airport billboards, advertisements in the hotels executives frequented, articles in hotel magazines (yes, people do read them) with tailored messaging, sponsored sporting events, banner ads on local search sites in towns executives frequently visited, and media coverage in targeted regional publications, to name some of the activities. Together with Sales, Marketing developed a plan on how follow-up would be handled and set metrics to determine what worked and what didn't.

That level of partnership between Sales and Marketing is what alignment is all about. Both teams are aligned to the Buyer, working towards a common goal with shared metrics and a common understanding of available resources. The constant communication between Sales and Marketing enabled the two teams to quickly assess what worked, refine activities to be more effective, and determine which programs to drop. Sales began to understand and appreciate the lead times involved in Marketing, like securing a billboard or advertorial in a magazine. Marketing began to understand the stress that Sales is under as they try to make quota. Both teams developed a healthy appreciation for how their differences were complementary.

Mending Burned Bridges

The showdown between sales and marketing has been epic. But it's clearly time to put aside all those hard feelings and start working with our marketing teams.

Where does Christine suggest we start? She says that reorganizing sales and marketing departments does not produce alignment; a cultural and structural change does. And it all begins with checking our assumptions about each other at the door. "Salespeople need to accept that just because their success enables the company to meet payroll doesn't mean they run the company," says Christine. "Likewise, marketers need to get their heads out of the creative clouds and walk several miles in the shoes of sales."

Reorganizing sales and marketing departments does not produce alignment; a cultural and structural change does. And it all begins with checking our assumptions about each other at the door.

According to Christine, the problem is that marketing leaders and CEOs often fail to specifically spell out for sales what their obligations are in alignment. "It's no wonder that marketing becomes frustrated with sales and that sales, in turn, doesn't understand why marketing can't deliver what they need to win deals."

According to Christine, there are only a handful of things that sales "must do" to make alignment work:

1. **Give up your customers.** Sales might have found, nurtured, and closed the customer, but to build a long-

term, productive customer relationship and company champion, you can't own that relationship. Once you've closed the deal, introduce marketing and customer service to the client. They take on the responsibility of making the customer successful and reference-able, and ferret out additional opportunities or naysayers.

2. **Ask marketing to schedule quarterly "check-ins"** to discuss the status of your customers and to develop a joint-account plan. It'll increase your add-on sales potential without any work on your part.

3. **Stop playing the blame game.** Everyone loses deals. Post-loss or post-win analyses, or blaming the prospect for the loss, hurts the whole company. Get over it.

Turn Your Clients Into Your Own, Private Sales Force

I agree with Christine on many points. But there's one where I vehemently disagree. As a salesperson, I would *never* "give up" my clients. Marketing and customer service both have roles to play after deals are closed. However, salespeople have significant relationships within client accounts. And we know that clients make buying decisions based on personal relationships.

More importantly, clients are your best (and often most untapped) source of new business. They already know and trust you, and they believe in your ability to deliver results. After all, *they* choose to do business with you. If you're not asking them for referrals, you're leaving money on the table—every single day.

SECTION 7

REFERRALS ROCK!

Sales is the best job in the world, but it's not an easy one. Only 63 percent of sales reps met quota in 2012, according to the CSO Insights Sales Performance Optimization (SPO) study,[50] the same number as the previous year. But while achievement of sales quotas has remained flat year over year, revenue targets have increased.

There's a big problem here. We're failing to make quota in large numbers, and yet management continues to increase sales goals.

In the same report, almost half of sales execs said that enhancing lead generation is their top initiative. Of course it is. But focusing simply on "lead generation" can take you down a rabbit hole of unproductive, inefficient prospecting strategies.

The key is to generate more *qualified* leads, which are the only ones that really count. The rest are a waste of our sales time. So how do you fill your sales pipeline with nothing but hot, qualified leads?

---

[50] CSO Insights, "CSO Insights Sales Performance Optimization (SPO) Study," http://www.csoinsights.com/Publications/Shop/Sales-Performance-Optimization (2013).

Marketing is not the answer. And neither is technology or social media. Referrals are the answer.

Referral selling is, hands down, the most effective and efficient prospecting strategy, because it addresses the two biggest challenges sales organizations face:

- Getting every meeting at the level that counts
- Converting prospects into customers

Consider your own selling experience. When you've received an introduction to exactly the person you want to meet, you:

- Arrive pre-sold—the prospect knows who you are and actually wants to meet you
- Gain trust and credibility—the most difficult (and important) criteria in the sales process
- Shorten your sales process—and spend more time working with great clients
- Ace out the competition—while others are still identifying the decision-makers
- Incur no hard costs—except, perhaps, the price of coffee or lunch for two
- Convert prospects into clients more than 50 percent of the time—and most people say more than 70 percent of the time

> The key is to generate more *qualified* leads, which are the only ones that really count. The rest are a waste of our sales time.

No other sales or marketing strategy comes close to these results.

When I interviewed sales and marketing executives for this book, I expected most of them to extol the virtues of technology and to downplay the role of human interaction in sales. Was I ever wrong! Even the marketing-automation and social-media experts agree that nothing beats the results we get with a qualified referral introduction.

This section is not a primer for referral selling. I already wrote that book—*No More Cold Calling*. And every word in it is still just as true today as it was then. However, I would be remiss to write a book about sales without including at least a brief overview of the most effective and productive prospecting strategy that exists. (Maybe you'll pick up a tip you've forgotten about and start reaping the rewards of referral selling.)

While globalization and rapid developments in technology make the world seem larger and more impersonal than ever, the truth is that people crave connections with one another. Most buyers conduct research before signing on the dotted line. But whether they need a new accountant, marketing firm, lawyer, technology solution, or bank, they don't pick one at random. They ask people they trust who *they* trust.

You don't have to take my word for it. A Nielsen study revealed that 90 percent of consumers trust their peers far more than ads.[51] Granted, this was a consumer study, but the same logic easily applies to B2B as well.

---

[51] *Nielsen*, "Global Advertising Consumers Trust Real Friends and Virtual Strangers the Most," http://www.nielsen.com/us/en/newswire/2009/global-advertising-consumers-trust-real-friends-and-virtual-strangers-the-most.html (July 7, 2009).

Ernie Almonte, chief visionary officer and CEO at Almonte Group, LLC, says, "All things being equal, we work with friends. All things not being equal, we work with friends. And when we need a specialist, we ask a friend."

Yet, despite the overwhelming evidence—both statistical and anecdotal—showing that referrals are the best way to work, 95 percent of companies don't have a systematic, disciplined referral program with goals, metrics, and accountability. Puzzling? It is to me.

"All things being equal, we work with friends. All things not being equal, we work with friends. And when we need a specialist, we ask a friend."

Referral selling is a strategic initiative driven by the executive team. It's part skills, part metrics, part process, part coaching, and part compensation. But the most important piece is the commitment from sales leaders to do what it takes to implement a referral system. (Check out my Referral I.Q. Quiz.[52] It's a 13-question evaluation that takes less than three minutes to complete.)

It's time to make referral selling your business-development priority—to establish metrics, integrate asking for referrals into your sales process, and build the skills to confidently ask for introductions to your ideal clients.

[52] http://www.nomorecoldcalling.com/download.html

REFERRALS: BY THE NUMBERS

Until recently, there was little hard data to back up my claims that referral selling is the most effective way to sell and that no one should ever have to cold call. However, there are now several studies proving I've been on the right track all this time.

For a report released by the Wharton School of Business,[53] researchers studied data that an anonymous German bank gathered on nearly 10,000 of its customers over 33 months. Their findings: Referred customers generated 16 to 25 percent more value than non-referred customers with similar demographics and time of acquisition. Referred clients also:

- Contributed higher margins (on average, 4.5 cents more per day, though this erodes over time)
- Were 13 percent more likely to stay with the company (a difference that persists over time)

In my own research, I've seen even more impressive results. I recently polled 1,100 sales professionals: 52 percent said that when they receive a qualified referral, they convert a sales prospect into

---

[53] Philip Schmitt, Bernd Skiera and Christophe Van den Bulte, "Referral Programs and Customer Value," Wharton School of Business, 2011.

a new client more than 70 percent of the time. And 31 percent said the conversion rate is more than 50 percent of the time.

> I recently polled 1,100 sales professionals: 52 percent said that when they receive a qualified referral, they convert a sales prospect into a new client more than 70 percent of the time. And 31 percent said the conversion rate is more than 50 percent of the time.

Let's do the math. We'll assume a 50-percent close rate and that only half of your contacts offer introductions when asked. Maybe some of your referral sources can't think of anyone right now, or perhaps you haven't been clear enough in describing exactly who you want to meet. Whatever the reason, if only half of the people you ask provide introductions, the results are still impressive:

- Ask 20 contacts for referral introductions.
- Receive 10 referral introductions to ideal clients.
- Schedule eight referral meetings.
- Book four new clients.

Wouldn't this make referral selling worth your time? The business results are more than compelling—even without taking into account the other benefits of referral selling, including:

- Increased deal size
- Shorter sales process
- Lower cost of sales

- New clients who become referral sources and help you generate even more new business

Many sales leaders I interviewed for this book had their own referral-selling data to share. According to Tom Miller, former vice president of channel management at Sage (U.K.) Ltd., his company conducted a customer survey to identify who influenced Sage partners the most in buying decisions. Not surprisingly, two major components (both related to referrals) accounted for more than half of their sales:

- Business partners—26 percent

- Their CPAs—25 percent

Yet, Tom was amazed that when he asked partners how they generated new business, many had no relationships with CPA firms in their own markets. "You don't establish relationships with a phone call," he says. "It takes time, and the client must recognize value."

Marge Bieler, CEO of RareAgent and social media and content manager at GT Software, offers a similar perspective. She has found that building a referral pipeline enables her team to work fewer leads with much shorter sales cycles. "Salespeople need conversations that convert into cash," she says. "The best way to get those conversations is by utilizing a trusted network of peers, partners, analysts, and clients who can refer us."

Marge says that when connections are made by this trusted network, her team's close rate is 45-percent higher than with non-referred business. Looking back at the last few years, *before and after* her company added marketing automation, 80 percent of their customer base came from referrals, and only 20 percent from marketing and SEO campaigns.

Greg Brush, senior vice president of sales at InsideView, told me repeatedly that a referral sale is worth 10 times that of a sale generated through any other prospecting strategy.

> "Salespeople need conversations that convert into cash," she says. "The best way to get those conversations is by utilizing a trusted network of peers, partners, analysts, and clients who can refer us."

Whether we're talking about accredited studies or specific anecdotes like these, the conclusion is always the same: Referral business is the most effective lead-generation strategy. Nothing else comes close.

Still, companies and salespeople continue to waste time and resources by relying on methods that rarely work—namely, cold calling.

Are You Hot or Cold?

I usually don't spend much time bashing cold calling. I prefer to focus on what *does* work—referral selling. But I don't believe anyone should ever have to cold call, and whenever I read a blog or an article on this unproductive prospecting strategy, it sends me over the top.

Recently, a blogger shared 10 tips for making better cold calls. In the first sentence, she described cold calling as a game. Let's be clear: Sales is not a game. It is a profession—a serious profession that requires skill and confidence. And cold calling wastes both your time and talent.

Cold calling is any attempt to contact someone who doesn't know you and doesn't expect to hear from you—by phone, email, social media, or the old-fashioned knocking on doors. Thus, buying lists pretty much amounts to cold calling; you're paying for names of people who aren't expecting, and don't really want to take, your call.

There's No Such Thing as a "Warm" Call

Salespeople often tell me they're not cold calling; they're making *warm* calls. The most recent version of the warm-call fantasy goes like this: You've researched prospects on social media, identified trigger events, gathered information from social intelligence, and checked their websites and blogs. Aha! Now you send them purposeful emails making the business case for why they should talk to you. You really believe you're not cold calling, because you know all about the prospects. You're sending a "warm" email, right?

Wrong! There's no such thing as a warm email, a warm phone call, or a warm knock on the door. If you don't have an introduction, your lead is freezing cold—even though you mistakenly think you've been able to avoid sounding like a pesky telemarketer.

A call is either cold or hot. And a call is only hot when you receive a referral introduction.

There's no such thing as a warm email, a warm phone call, or a warm knock on the door. If you don't have an introduction, your lead is freezing cold—even though you mistakenly think you've been able to avoid sounding like a pesky telemarketer.

Everyone Hates Cold Calling

In a survey of 1,226 sales professionals,[54] respondents ranked the prospect of making cold calls for a week as more unappealing than giving up sex for a month! The only activity they found more unattractive was getting a root canal.

Buyers hate getting cold calls as much, if not more, than salespeople hate making them. According to a survey by Huthwaite:

---

[54] *Reuters*, "Making cold calls? People would rather give up sex," http://www.reuters.com/article/2010/05/19/us-workplace-sales-idUSTRE64I5QC20100519 (May 19, 2010).

- 91 percent never respond to an unsolicited inquiry.
- 71 percent find cold calls annoying.
- 88 percent will have nothing to do with cold callers.
- 94 percent can't remember a single prospector or product received during the last two years.

Cold emails are just as bad. These annoying, impersonal, nonspecific, and unsolicited messages clog up my Inbox and drive me nuts. Below is an example of the kind of emails I regularly receive—a great example of what NOT to do:

> *Hi there,* (What happened to the personal salutation? My first name isn't "there.")
>
> *Would you be interested in acquiring any of the updated contact databases of below specified titles that will add great value to your marketing programs?* (No.)
>
> *We provide contacts of all level executive titles (C- Level, VP-level, Director-level, Manager-level and other executives). We would be happy to customize the list accordingly, if you have any other specific requirements.* (Of course you'd be happy. I wouldn't.)
>
> *I imagine that you're most likely flooded with such emails from several "so called' list providers.* (I sure am.) *However, we are a legitimate company that has been in existence for more than 8 years now and a strong competitor to companies like D&B, Harte Hanks and Zoom info.* (So what?)
>
> *We have your market covered.* (How do you know my market?)

> *We can help you learn from industry best practices, and our experience with thousands of clients that we have deployed, so you achieve the best possible results. With more than 140 million decision makers around the globe, you are sure to reach your next customer.* (I have a better way of reaching decision-makers. You have no idea how out of touch you sound.)

You probably get tons of these emails (which pretty much amount to spam), and I'd be willing to bet that you—like me—delete most or all of them without even bothering to respond, right? After all, do you really want to hear from people who don't even know your name? Clearly they haven't put much time or effort into reaching you.

Salespeople often tell me they're *required* to make 100 dials a day. If they're lucky, they might get 20 people on the phone, set eight appointments, and perhaps close one deal. That's a 1-percent return on your time investment. Yikes!

Whether you're buying lists, sending direct mail, dropping off brochures at company headquarters (yes, that still happens), or sending spam email to people who don't know you and don't want to hear from you, it all amounts to cold calling—the bane of a salesperson's existence.

REFERRAL TRAPS

Salespeople and sales executives agree that referrals are the No. 1 way to attract and retain top clients. Yet, few run a 100-percent referral business.

I find this puzzling. If referral prospecting is unsurpassable, why are the pros so passive about developing a disciplined referral system? It turns out that referral selling might be common sense, but it's not common practice.

Why We Don't Ask

I have discovered five reasons companies don't utilize their most powerful sales tool:

1. **Failure to prioritize.** Note that the word "priority" is singular. When you commit to referral selling, it becomes the way you work. Sales execs tell me the reason they don't ask for referrals is that they have other priorities. Really? What is more important than generating qualified leads, getting every meeting with decision-makers, closing deals, and generating revenue? The truth is that we waste hours a day on activities that don't deliver ROI. But referrals do.

2. **Lack of metrics.** Referral selling seems like a great prospecting approach, but many companies either believe that referrals are tough to measure, or they've never added referral metrics to their sales goals. Measure essential referral activities (e.g., the number of referral introductions requested, referrals received, and meetings conducted). Determine your referral revenue goals—such as percent revenue increase, number of new clients, or number of new projects. Set referral goals for your company and for each member of the sales team.

3. **No sales process.** Asking for referrals is a proactive strategy, to be nurtured and integrated into your sales process, not just left to word of mouth. Your work may speak for itself, but your clients probably won't ... unless you ask. After all, how much thought do you give to referring great contacts in your network unless someone or something brings them to your attention?

4. **Lack of skills/practice.** Most sellers don't ask for referral introductions with confidence. They've never learned a reliable process, so they say, "By the way, if you know anyone who could benefit from my services, please pass my name along." You may check "ask for a referral" off your to-do list this way. But even the most well-intentioned referral sources will think no more of this generic inquiry once distracted by their own hectic schedules.

> Your work may speak for itself, but your clients probably won't ... unless you ask.

5. **Personal discomfort.** From the newbie, to the seasoned sales pro, to the hard-driving sales executive, asking for referral introductions feels uncomfortable for most people. We worry that doing so could imply our businesses are struggling, and that asking already-busy people to help us might mean risking those relationships. Worst of all, they might say no. Unlike other business-development strategies, our reputations are clearly on the line.

Get Over It

That's the great thing about referrals. Everyone wins!

When your referral sources introduce you to new prospects, they're not just helping you; they're helping the people to whom they refer you as well. They introduce you—a credible resource—and save their associates the time they would have spent interviewing other vendors. Referrals are built on truth and integrity. Think of all the referrals you easily and willingly provide: You tell people about a great restaurant, a terrific movie, a top mechanic, or the latest iPad app you bought. And you don't consider it an imposition or a favor to do so. That's the great thing about referrals. Everyone wins!

No Excuses

Excuses like "I forget" or "It's not the right time" are other reasons people give for not asking—and these are red flags that indicate the downward spiral of never asking. We can always "forget" or justify that it's not the right time to approach someone, when we're really just uncomfortable. The easy part of shifting to referral selling is learning the skills, establishing metrics, and integrating it into your sales process and goal setting. For many people, the more difficult part is asking with confidence. Just remember, you give referrals all the time—and enjoy it. Why wouldn't others do the same for you? Of course they will! Just ask.

The NOW Mentality

Salespeople are not patient people. We want information now, not tomorrow or the next day. We want it quickly and magically. We'd prefer to put our iPods (loaded with critical sales tips and wisdom) under our pillows and awaken the next day with the essential sales content embedded in our brains. Osmosis would be such a low-impact, low-energy, easy way to master new sales skills ...

Snap out of it. That's not how it works, and you know it.

Salespeople in the top 10 percent operate differently. They're focused, energized, driven to provide top-notch products and services to clients, relentless, and always moving—learning, developing expertise, and asking questions. They do what's "closest to cash" first—every day. This could be writing a proposal, following up on a referral, returning a phone call, scheduling a meeting with a sales prospect, or asking for referral introductions.

It's time to move referral selling from common sense to common practice. Determine how these excuses for not asking play out in your company, and build a plan to shift the way you work. Your bottom line will never be the same.

When's the Right Time to Ask for Referrals?

Salespeople often ask me *when* they should ask for referrals. Many think they should wait until a client has signed a deal, or until their solution has been implemented. Others feel they can't ask until the client sees a significant ROI. We wait and we wait, often until the relationship with the initial buyer is so far removed that we never get around to it at all.

You've Earned the Right

So when should you ask? The short answer: When you've earned the right.

You've definitely earned the right when you've been referred, or at any point during the sales process when you add value. How will you know? Your clients thank you. You've given them an idea, shared an insight, introduced them to people they should know, or told the truth when it was difficult to do so. You've also earned the right with everyone you've gotten to know during the sales and implementation process.

Don't Lose the Right Once You've Earned It

Never lose touch with your contacts at client companies. Clients are our best sources of referrals—to other divisions of their companies and to their peers in other organizations.

> It's never too soon to ask clients for referrals. And it's never too late—as long as you have continued to stay in touch and nurture those relationships.

Far too many sales organizations are so focused on bringing in new business that they neglect their current customers. Doug Landis, vice president of productivity at Box, agrees. "A lot of companies focus more on the sale than post-sale," he says. "They're focused on sell-in and not sell-through. These companies don't last. Companies with the strongest sell-through teams have the biggest impact. So pick up the phone as often as you can."

Jim Mallory, director of marketing for e2b teknologies, also understands the importance of nurturing client relationships. He shared the following story with me:

> A few years ago, we started offering our customers a free, annual ERP check-up, which is basically time we set aside to visit with customers and find out what's new in their businesses. We discuss what's working for them and areas where they are challenged in respect to their business software. This activity has generated hundreds of thousands of dollars in revenue by simply touching our customers one time a year. During one of these check-ups, we asked for

> referrals, and the client introduced us to one of his largest customers. It took several months, but the referral paid off, and we closed the largest ERP deal in the history of our company.

Bottom line: It's never too soon to ask clients for referrals. And it's never too late—as long as you have continued to stay in touch and nurture those relationships.

So start asking. You'll get to walk straight into meetings with your ideal prospects—without cold calling or trying to figure out how to bypass the gatekeeper.

THE GATEKEEPER HAS LEFT THE BUILDING

You've probably read countless articles and blogs, and observed a dozen webinars or podcasts, telling you how to convince that pesky receptionist or assistant to grant you access to a decision-maker.

These "gatekeeper tactics" make my blood boil! They're insincere, duplicitous, unprofessional, offensive, and a waste of sales time—a waste of *your* time.

These gatekeepers are valuable to the executives they serve, but not to you—at least not until you've developed a relationship. And certainly not when you cold call.

Technology won't help you get past the gatekeeper and into important meetings. As Rich Dorfman, partner and vice president of client and professional services for Convergent Computing, puts it, "Technology is very good at qualifying. But it's not good at getting us in front of the right person. Getting to the decision-maker is highly dependent on personal connections and referrals."

If you've been introduced by a trusted source, these gatekeepers will *welcome* your call. The secret isn't duping them (trust me, they're onto you). It's being a call they expect. In fact, when you receive a referral, there is no gatekeeper. This person has a new title: Your Referral Advocate.

Consider the following story veteran salesman George Springer told me while working as a sales and service engineer at Greenleaf Corporation:

> I had a customer with whom I'd been working for several years. I had written some business with him, but it was a struggle to get through their inertia and create new business. They kept putting me off with the typical "stall" tactics.
>
> My upper-management team and our top engineers were visiting from headquarters, and I was setting up appointments as they made a swing through the Southeast. But I was struggling to arrange a meeting with this particular customer. One engineer couldn't make it, and another was out on medical leave. The only available engineer was a great guy but not really a decision-maker. I was ready to give up.
>
> Instead, I asked him for help finding attendees. This helpful engineer got involved and contacted more employees at his site. In the end, I had at least nine engineering and production staff members for our meeting—all new leads. We closed business and opened the door to more opportunities we didn't have before.

What a great lesson! Not only was there no gatekeeper, but George initiated a sales process that his competitors didn't even know about.

Building a relationship with someone on the inside—even if it's someone who can't authorize a deal—amounts to a referral, and an effective one at that. Eighty-four percent of executives say they *usually* or *always* accept calls from salespeople who have been recommended internally, according to *Selling to the C-Suite* by Nicholas A.C. Read and Dr. Stephen J. Bistritz.[55]

> If you've been introduced by a trusted source, these gatekeepers will *welcome* your call. The secret isn't duping them (trust me, they're onto you). It's being a call they expect.

So stop worrying about sneaking past the gatekeeper. When you receive a referral introduction, that dreaded middleman is no longer an obstacle. In fact, he might just be your new best friend.

[55] Nicholas A.C. Read and Stephen J. Bistritz, *Selling to the C-Suite: What Every Executive Wants You to Know About Successfully Selling to the Top*, McGraw-Hill, 2009.

You Don't Know Who Your Neighbor Knows

Your clients—current and former—are your best, most logical source of referrals. They know how you work, what your ideal client looks like, and how you add value. But while they make up the top tier of your referral network, there is untapped potential for new leads in every area of your life. And thanks to technology, you're now connected to more referral sources than ever.

We've all heard of "Six Degrees of Separation"—a theory posited by psychologist Stanley Milgram in a 1967 study, for which 296 volunteers from Boston and Nebraska attempted to get a document to a Massachusetts stockbroker using only their acquaintances. Sixty-four of those letters reached the stockbroker after going through six connected people.

Today, thanks to the internet and social media, we don't need six people to connect us to Kevin Bacon or anyone else. New research shows it now takes fewer than five. A 2011 study by Facebook and the University of Milan, which mined data from the social-media site's 721 million active users, found that the number of intermediate links between two strangers—better known as degrees of separation—is now only 4.74. Researchers summarize: "When considering another person in the world, on average, a friend of your friend knows a friend of their friend."

This is great news for referral sellers! We're connected to any decision-maker we want to reach by just a few people.

The World Is Your Oyster

Many of us believe that, because our businesses are super-complex and sophisticated, only certain people are worthwhile connections. This assumption is plain wrong. Everyone knows someone.

Referrals come from everywhere. Think of all the people you know. All those people know other people. And you don't know *who* they know until you ask. You might get the perfect referral from your attorney, another passenger on an airplane, your fellow employees, your next-door neighbor, or even your family.

Don't Count Anyone Out

I've been surprised time and time again by the people others know. We readily stereotype people. We judge them by their age, their job positions, the way they dress, the way they speak, and the cars they drive. It's called First Impression Management. The good news is that when we're right, it saves time; but when we're wrong, we miss out on opportunities.

Before I founded No More Cold Calling, I worked for a consulting firm. One day, as I was telling a colleague that I was having a difficult time connecting with the vice president of sales at a high-tech company, a new IT employee overheard my conversation and said he might be able to help. "Oh sure," I thought. "He's just an IT guy." But that IT guy taught me an important lesson: No one should be discounted when it comes to your referral network. It turns out that his mother was the executive assistant for exactly the man I wanted to meet. She made the introduction, and I got the appointment.

The Power of the Water Cooler

Some of your best potential referral sources are the people you see every day—your co-workers. Everyone in your organization knows hundreds of other people. Who do you think understands the value of your organization better than your colleagues? And who could possibly have more invested in your company's success? Referrals are right under your nose.

Where did your colleagues work *before* they joined your company? Who are their next-door neighbors? Who were their college roommates? Perhaps one of them has a brother who works at your prospect company. Spend time talking to the people who work for and with you. Learn about their histories and what's important to them. Help them understand what drives you and the best way to share referrals.

Don't assume you know who people know. Just ask. If you don't ask, you don't get.

Referrals often come from the most unexpected sources, which is why we should always be asking—everyone, not just those who seem to make the most sense.

Don't assume you know who people know. Just ask. If you don't ask, you don't get.

To Incent, or Not to Incent

There are two kinds of incentives companies provide for referrals: Incentives for referral sources and incentives for salespeople who bring in new clients through referrals.

Sales leaders frequently ask whether they should provide incentives to referral sources. The short answer is no. On the other hand, giving incentives to salespeople is a great idea!

Your Referral Reputation

> Referrals are far more powerful when they're meant to simply connect people who can benefit from knowing each other—not when they're given in exchange for kickbacks.

So why shouldn't you give incentives to referral sources?

Think about it. When you refer someone, your reputation is on the line. You refer people you know and trust to take care of your clients or colleagues just as well as you would. When someone offers to pay me for a referral, I run the other way. Referrals are far more powerful when they're meant to simply connect people who can benefit from knowing each other—not when they're given in exchange for kickbacks.

If you choose to send a small gift or to make a charitable donation after the fact, that's fine. Just don't make compensation the reason people refer you.

In Wharton's study of the German bank's referral program,[56] the organization did offer incentives to customers who referred new clients. However, the researchers admit that while such company-stimulated, word-of-mouth programs (WOM) attract more clients, they are ultimately less effective than organic referrals. These authors point to several studies that have determined the shortfalls of referral programs that offer incentives. Here are some of the findings:

- Such efforts often involve a monetary reward for the referrer who, as a result, may seem less trustworthy.
- Programs providing economic benefits tend not to be very sustainable.
- Unlike organic WOM, stimulated WOM is not free, raising questions about cost-effectiveness.
- In most referral programs, the reward is given regardless of how long the new referred customers stay with the firm. This incentive structure creates the potential for abuse in which existing customers get rewarded for referring low-quality customers.

---

[56] Philip Schmitt, Bernd Skiera, and Christophe Van den Bulte, "Referral Programs and Customer Value," Wharton School of Business, 2011.

While incentive programs may work in some cases, a *genuine* referral from a client, just because the person trusts you and is invested in helping you, provides a much greater return in the long run.

While I don't recommend incenting clients to refer you, I have found it valuable to have referral-based partnerships with organizations that target similar demographics. These partnerships are formal contracts and, in several cases, mutual agreements—where partners agree to refer you. These agreements are based on a simple premise: Make a referral and receive compensation when business closes. I currently have such agreements with several companies. I commit to these partnerships because I believe in what these companies have to offer. Even so, whenever I recommend them, I always disclose our business relationship. I simply make introductions, tell my clients and colleagues about my good experience, and then let them decide if it's a fit for them.

Their Referral Reward

What about incenting salespeople? You bet you should. There's practically no cost associated with referral selling. It takes your sales team less time to close deals. They score important meetings right off the bat, and they develop deep, lasting relationships that most likely wouldn't have happened without referrals.

I'm not an incentive specialist (though I'd be glad to refer you to experts who are). However, here's my point of view. A referral spiff on a closed referral deal is No. 1. You should be thrilled to write that check!

You might also consider incenting activities that *lead to* referral sales—such as referral introductions requested, referral introductions made, and referral meetings completed. In order to make referral selling work, your team must systematically identify sources and

> What about incenting salespeople? You bet you should.

ask for introductions. So why not reward that behavior?

Incentives take many shapes—from financial rewards, to praise, to gifts. You can acknowledge referral accomplishments with a group voicemail or email, or by making announcements in weekly meetings. You might also opt to give bonuses, gift cards for movies, dinners, luxury products, and vacations.

You may be thinking that salespeople are paid to sell. So why should you incent them? After all, they should know that referrals are the fast track to higher commissions. "Should" is the operative word here. There's lots we "should" do, but we often don't—unless we have goals, accountability, and rewards. It's human nature.

I thought I didn't care about awards. When I worked for Omega Performance, we had lots of awards. In my first year, I won Rookie of the Year and Bias for Action. I won a spot in our awards trip four years in a row. As a member of the elite Paladin Club, I received a carved crystal paperweight on an elegant engraved base. That was in 1992. I've moved my office several times in the intervening years, but I can't bring myself to toss it. That award is still in a prominent place in my office. (Confession: I've turned the base around so the engraving doesn't show, but I know it's there.)

Incent or not. It's your choice. I've given you my point of view. But whichever route you take, always remember to thank your referral sources.

Mom Was Right—Manners Matter

A thank-you goes a long way—thanks for a referral, thanks for new business, thanks for the meeting.

You can never thank someone enough. Not only is it a great way to show appreciation, but it's also a great reason to follow up and nurture relationships with people in your referral network.

Your Referral Sources Want to Know

Your referral sources want to know when they've made a perfect referral. Once they know what you need, more referrals will follow. In fact, when people send me referrals, I often thank them several times throughout the sales process—immediately upon receiving the referral, again when I know the outcome of the referral, and again when the check comes in.

Your Clients Want to Know

Thank your new clients for their business and show your appreciation. Not only is this a professional way to work and build relationships, but it keeps you top of mind for your clients—the premier source of referrals to others just like them.

Phone, email, in person—these are terrific ways to express gratitude. But if you really want to impress, there's nothing like an old-fashioned, handwritten note.

Thank-You Notes Are Not Passé

Phone, email, in person—these are terrific ways to express gratitude. But if you really want to impress, there's nothing like an old-fashioned, handwritten note.

Sending a thank-you card shows you actually *care enough* to take the time, energy, and focus to locate the card and postage stamp, put it all together, and get it to the mailbox. Our world is connected, electronic, wireless, character-limited, and immediate. This has made communication easy. But a casual, off-the-cuff email or text doesn't communicate, "You are worth my real time."

Not Saying "Thank You" Says a Lot

Maybe I'm from another planet. I was taught that when you receive a gift, you say thank you. It's polite and respectful. I personally autograph and give my *No More Cold Calling* book to many people--colleagues, clients, friends, and prospects. I rarely receive a thank-you.

What message does that send? To me, it says these salespeople don't follow through. I think twice about giving them referrals. If they don't follow through with me, how will they treat my clients?

In her blog post, "Send Me a Thank You Note—Pretty Please,"[57] bestselling author and networking expert Susan RoAne writes,

---

[57] Susan RoAne, "Send Me a Thank You Note – Pretty Please!," http://susanroane.com/send-me-a-thank-you-note-pretty-please/ (July 16, 2009).

"To paraphrase a professor I know, 'If you have the time to eat the meal that I cooked and/or paid for, you have the five minutes to let me know you valued my efforts.'"

For the sake of basic decency, remember to thank people who help you. Otherwise, you may eventually find that not many people are eager to lend you their support.

THE FORTUNE'S IN YOUR FOLLOW-UP

As a successful sales professional, you meet a lot of people—at sales conferences, trade shows, and networking events. You have clients, business partners, colleagues, former colleagues, and all sorts of people in your referral network.

While you certainly can't meet all of these people for coffee each week, you *can* find ways to follow up on a regular basis so that you stay on their referral radar. Here are just a few ideas:

- **Mine your database**. There's no excuse for failing to follow up. Use your database to record relevant contact information and provide a tickler for your next conversation. I'm horrified when salespeople tell me they've actually received referrals and haven't followed up. (I know that's not you.)

- **Engage in social media.** Social media is not a place to sell, but it is a place to pose questions, answer questions, and communicate valuable information—not only from you, but also from other credible sources.

- **Write a blog.** Keep them short, and post at least weekly. I'm sure you're not at a loss for something to say about your industry or information to share that would be relevant to your clients. Link your blog directly to LinkedIn so your contacts see when you post.

- **Send articles.** Sharing relevant, interesting content with your network is a great way to stay in touch and provide value. You can write your own or get other authors' permission to use their articles (with attribution).

- **Write newsletters.** Reach out at least quarterly with a newsletter—something a little meatier than your short weekly blogs. The newsletter is not about you; it's about your readers. What insights can you share? Lessons learned?

You could also profile a client you helped. Describe the *situation* or problem the client faced, summarize the *solution* you provided, and then demonstrate the *results* your client received. Quantify the results as much as possible by describing how much money the company saved, the newfound security of the client's investments, or the risk you helped diminish. We all love and listen to good stories.

- **Solicit feedback.** Part of keeping your customers happy—and, therefore, more likely to give you repeat business and to refer others—is communicating, not just during the sales process but also during and after implementation. Check in regularly to find out what they're delighted about, apprehensive about, or don't understand. This level of communication—and your genuine concern for their entire customer experience—builds trust, alleviates any anxiety, and provides them with a degree of control, clarity, and confidence.

- **Show appreciation.** We've already covered this one, but it's important enough to merit repeating. Take any opportunity to thank those who have helped you in some way. It's not only good manners; it's a great excuse to reach out and nurture valuable sales relationships.

You never know when people are ready to buy or how something you say will resonate at just the right time. So stay in touch. In sales, timing is everything. Referrals are everything. And the fortune is in *your* follow-up!

A Special Message for CPAs

"I don't work with CPA firms."

That's what I told the managing partners of 40 prestigious CPA firms. Why? Because in my experience, CPAs understand and acknowledge that referrals are the best way to engage new clients. Yet, they don't commit to implementing a referral program—even when they can quantify the results in black and white. They don't make the time, because it's always the 15th of some month (typical tax deadlines in the U.S.).

Leaders at these firms point to their managers and say "train them." This baffles me. It's not about training "them." It's about changing how the entire firm thinks about and approaches business development. Most partners haven't adopted a consistent, measurable referral system. Sure, they get referrals from time to time, and most have terrific connections with bankers, attorneys, and insurance professionals. The problem is that every firm has the same great connections, so these relationships don't really provide a competitive advantage—*unless* your firm is one of the few that *actively* works to generate referrals.

The irony is that clients will always take calls from their CPAs. CPAs have built-in meetings with their clients, which is a huge, untapped advantage. They have frequent opportunities to ask clients for referrals. Yet, when I ask CPA leaders if they have a clear, consistent process for asking current clients for referrals, the answer is almost always no.

In a recent poll of managing partners, here's what I learned:

- Partners weren't consistently asking clients for referrals and didn't have a disciplined referral system.
- More than 80 percent said their partners and staff didn't have requisite skills and were not comfortable asking for referrals.

Frightening, isn't it? Most CPAs think "sales" is like a four-letter word. The prevailing attitude seems to be: "I didn't become a CPA to sell. Just let me do the work, and if I do good work for my clients, they'll refer me." And so it goes … nothing changes.

I have a CPA client (let's call her Ellen) who's become a friend and colleague. Ellen is a partner in her firm and an expert in her field. She has a dynamic personality and connects with people immediately. Once you meet her, you trust her. I offered to work one-on-one with Ellen to help build her practice.

> Those in professional services are just as capable of building referral-selling strategies as any of us. But they have a harder time shaking their negative biases about sales—and they don't make referrals a priority.

I vividly recall one particular conversation. It was the end of July, and we were finishing up a wonderful dinner. I asked Ellen about her business-development plans. She said identifying new clients was her focus for the next two months—August and September. But when I asked about her specific plan, I learned she didn't have one. That wasn't OK with me. I dug in.

I asked Ellen if she had contacted her current clients and asked them for referrals. Suddenly this remarkable, vibrant woman slumped in her chair, looked at me, and said in a meek voice, "Do I have to?"

Later, I joined Ellen for a breakfast meeting with one of her long-time clients. Prior to the meeting, she and I discussed her goal (what she wanted to walk away with) and my role in guiding the discussion.

Over breakfast, much of the conversation was about reconnecting, travels, and wine. As the conversation turned to business, the client mentioned some resources he was looking for in his business. Turns out, Ellen had a perfect company to recommend. She then asked him for a referral. He had two ideas and offered to introduce Ellen to both contacts. Mission accomplished—and a "win" for both parties.

Those in professional services are just as capable of building referral-selling strategies as any of us. But they have a harder time shaking their negative biases about sales—and they don't make referrals a priority.

Partners at these firms tell me it's critical to develop the next generation of rainmakers. Many of these leaders are Baby Boomers and plan to retire in a few years. So I decided to find out just how serious they were about referral selling.

At the end of May, I sent the following email to this same group of managing partners, with the subject line "Referral Busy Season Begins August 1":

Dear (First Name),

When we last spoke, you were interested in building a referral discipline in your practice. You asked me to follow up with you. Then came your busy season. Then vacation.

Why Now

If you're serious about building a referral practice, we need to discuss your situation before the end of June. The time to initiate a referral program is August 1. Otherwise, you face October 15 deadlines and end-of-year planning, and then it's busy season again. If we don't start now, another year will go by.

The best time to equip partners, managers, and staff with referral strategies and skills is before busy season. Many people in your firm meet with clients during that time, and you leave money on the table if you're not asking clients to introduce you to people they know.

Your Role

Referral selling is a strategic initiative that must be driven by you and implemented within your firm. Marketing does an excellent job, and your business developer has a role, but it's the responsibility of everyone in your firm to leverage the great relationships they have built.

Schedule a Call

Here are dates and times for a 30-minute conference call.

I added a list of possible meeting times and sent the email to the partners I'd met and spoken with on the phone. I heard back from two people. One said her firm was going to pass. The other said he would send my email to the CEO to see if he was interested. Of course, I never heard anything.

My message to CPAs: You know referrals work. Not sure where to begin? Start by reading my first book, *No More Cold Calling®: The Breakthrough System That Will Leave Your Competition in the Dust*. Are you ready to commit to doing what it takes to build a strong referral practice in your firm? You decide. If so, please contact me at joanne@nomorecoldcalling.com or 415-461-8763.

CONCLUSION

NO TOYS AT THE TABLE

Selling is the Best Job in the World

We can solve problems for our clients, be instrumental in growing their businesses, engage in robust discussions, expand their thinking, and build amazing relationships. No other job gives us the opportunity to truly connect with people and plug into the pulse of the economy from anywhere in the world.

Selling is personal—very, very personal. We need to be present, involved, and connected. We need to connect—one human being to the other. It's then that we can make the person-to-person sale. Technology is a support for our sales process, not a substitute.

You'll need to get connected and stay connected. We're all linked to technology more than ever before. Many of us spend more time talking on our cell phones, checking email, or showing off the bells and whistles of our latest gadget, than we do actually connecting with people, especially new people.

Sound familiar? I wrote these exact words in 2006 in Chapter One of my first book, *No More Cold Calling*. Some things never change. Relationships still rule in sales. There's a direct correlation between your personal connections and your sales success.

In 2013, I read *Successful Social Selling*,[58] by Matt Heinz, president of Heinz Marketing. With his permission, I'd like to share a portion of the introduction with you:

> Technology has a habit of making our personal interactions less intimate, less meaningful, more uniform. The volumes of people we can connect with now via email, Twitter, other social networks is great at scale, but superficial in creating the kind of bonds and relationships that have historically driven preference and decisions in the business world.
>
> And despite the proliferation of electronic networking channels, we still make decisions based on decidedly offline and personal criteria. We prefer to do business with people we like, people we trust. And although relationships can be fostered and extended via online means, they are created and converted most typically in a far more traditional fashion.
>
> So it's interesting to me that we see so many new technologies being built to help us better tap into and "reconnect" with the deeply personal and offline nature of relationship-building and sales acceleration.

---

[58] Matt Heinz, *Successful Social Selling*, Heinz Marketing Press, 2012.

> LinkedIn can only go so far. It fails to effectively differentiate a strong connection from a weak one. It doesn't say anything about offline bonds, family and social connections, let alone relationships that haven't been proactively entered and documented in the channel.
>
> And it's interesting to me that what we're using technology to try and reach, is what our parents and past generations did so well without any of this.
>
> Five hours on the golf course may be inefficient. It may not scale. But it worked then, and it works now.
>
> Relationships, as well as sales, are personal. We can use technology to more effectively identify and leverage opportunities, but consummation will always be more about what's happening in our hearts and minds.

Matt hit the nail on the head. Never forget that we ultimately do business with individuals, not with companies. Yes, you should do your research and use tech tools that increase your knowledge. Then stop. Your connection is not technology. Your connection is a person, just like you.

This lesson applies to every area of your life. Help your kids understand what a real person looks like. It's not an avatar, not a game, and not a text. They won't know the value of conversation and the importance of relationships unless you teach them by example. Bring back dinner conversation. No toys at the table. Nothing on our devices is so important it can't wait.

Never forget that we ultimately do business with individuals, not with companies.

As for your sales career, pick up the damn phone and talk to your prospects and clients! If you don't, someone else will.

It's never too soon (or too late) to ask for referrals, to help someone, to contribute, to say thanks, or just to catch up. Step out from behind the technology curtain and discover the real world. It's waiting for you.

NOTE FROM THE AUTHOR

"A truly good book teaches me better than to read it. I must soon lay it down, and commence living on its hint. What I began by reading, I must finish by acting."

—HENRY DAVID THOREAU

The measure of a book's success is not how many people buy it, but how many people use it to improve their lives. Henry Miller was once asked what brings a book to life. His simple response:

> A book lives through the passionate recommendation of one reader to another ... Like money, books must be kept in constant circulation. I leave you with two wishes: that you use this book actively and thoroughly to enhance your ability to present, and once you have attained this goal and enriched your mind, that you give a copy to someone else as a gift of the knowledge. You will be richer twice.

If you like this book and find it useful, please consider adding a review on Amazon and recommending it to your friends and colleagues. Thanks in advance for your support!

It's also worth pointing out that technology will continue to change and evolve. New terms will surface that we never heard of a few months ago. For instance, I just read about General Electric developing the "industrial Internet." As you draw conclusions from this book, please don't roll your eyes and think the information is "so last century" because terms change or are no longer "new." The names of the technology don't matter. You do. So make choices that matter—for your sales career, your family, and your life.

EXPERTS AND CONTRIBUTORS

A big thanks to all the sales experts and leaders I interviewed for this book. They were generous enough to share their time with me and to provide thoughtful responses to my questions about the links between sales, technology, and referrals. As you might expect, I met almost all of these people through referrals.

These contributors are arranged in the order they first appear in the book, although many people are mentioned more than once. I encourage you to check their websites, invite them to connect with you, and let them know what you think of their perspectives in Pick Up the Damn Phone!

Barry Trailer—Managing Partner and Co-Founder, CSO Insights

Barry and I are practically neighbors. We exchange ideas regularly. The research provided by CSO Insights is a "must have" for every sales exec.

Jim Blasingame—The Small Business Advocate; Author of *The Age of the Customer*

I contribute to Jim's Brain Trust, blog, and Internet radio show (5:30 a.m. Pacific). Jim is *the* small business advocate and a terrific colleague.

David Nour—Author of *Relationship Economics*

David makes the business case for building, nurturing, and expanding relationships (i.e., no relationships equals no sales).

Steve Woods—Group Vice President of Software Development, Oracle; former Chief Technology Officer, Eloqua

I wanted Steve's perspective on the role of marketing in relationship building. He even made time for me during the busy Oracle acquisition.

Jim Mallory—Director of Marketing, e2bteknologies

Jim knew his existing prospecting approaches were expensive and weren't working. Now, his company's referral results are remarkable.

David Satterwhite—Vice President of Worldwide Sales, Appcelerator; former Vice President of Sales and General Manager, Americas, Good Technology

David spoke at a Sales 2.0 Conference, and I asked for his perspective on the role of technology in sales.

Geoff Ashley— Principal, PROe; former Director of Business Development, SAP Americas

Geoff is a critical thinker. We exchange ideas and share frustrations about misdirected sales trends.

Brian Schlosser—Vice President of Global Accounts, Information Intelligence Group, EMC

Brian contributed great nuggets to my book, and he introduced me to my publisher, Booktrope.

Andy Paul—Author of *Zero-Time Selling*

We are two authors who share a similar vision. I'm always reminded that responsiveness matters.

Ian Brodie—Marketing Coach

I spoke with Ian, who is based in the U.K., to get a more global perspective on relationships and referrals.

Dawn Westerberg—Founder, Dawn Westerberg Consulting

Dawn's focus on marketing and my focus on sales are aligned. (Wow, this is one time sales doesn't hate marketing.)

Diane Updyke—Acting Vice President of Sales and Advisor for several sales-intelligence companies; former Vice President of Sales, Crowd Factory

I sat next to Diane at a conference and told her I loved her jewelry. (Yes, women do that.) We followed up with a call and an interview.

Russ Colombo—President and CEO, Bank of Marin

Russ and I met in person when I interviewed him for this book—one of only two face-to-face meetings. What a treat to learn first-hand about the power of relationships!

Craig Rosenberg—Co-Founder, TOPO

Craig's combination of sales and marketing expertise is unique and enlightening.

Bill Binch—Senior Vice President of Sales, Marketo

Bill interviewed me during a Dreamforce Conference. I asked him for an interview in return. His personal story is epic.

Evan Samurin—Partner Development Manager, Infusionsoft

I wanted the perspective of a 30-something about the power of relationships. Evan didn't let me down.

Ralf VonSosen—Head of Marketing and Sales Solutions, LinkedIn

Ralf was the perfect person with whom to discuss the connections between LinkedIn and referrals.

Todd McCormick—Senior Vice President of Sales, Silverpop

When I first heard Todd talk about seeing "the whites of their eyes," I knew we had to meet. He truly believes in "getting personal."

Cindy Bates—Vice President, U.S. SMB and Distribution, Microsoft

Cindy provides a big-company perspective on the integration of technology and sales.

Mike Hurst—Partner, HurstWorks Consulting

Insights from Mike's multi-cultural background blew me away.

George Papa—Vice President of Worldwide Sales, Altera Corporation

I interviewed George for my first book. The first time we met, he began the conversation with: "You're not a Yankees fan, are you?" If you know American baseball, you'll know George's favorite team.

Donal Daly—Founder and CEO, The TAS Group

Donal is off-the-charts smart and readily shared his wisdom. He provides a great dose of reality.

John Tellenbach—Senior Vice President, Comerica Bank

John shares unique perspectives about ways his bankers differentiate themselves.

Jonathan Farrington—CEO, JF Consultancy

Where do I start? I've known Jonathan for more than seven years, and he inducted me into the *Top Sales World* Hall of Fame. He is one of the most generous people I know.

Jeff Rosenthal—Senior Partner, Korn/Ferry Leadership and Talent Consulting Business

Jeff and I worked at the same company. He is a super connector, and we stay in touch to this day.

Jill Rowley—Social Selling Evangelist, Oracle; former Enterprise Sales Rep, Eloqua

Jill is the doyenne of social selling. "Social" *is* the way she works.

David Novak—Executive Vice President of Sales and Business Development, SPS Commerce

I was fascinated by David's business model, which is about relationships and partnering.

Dan Druker—Chief Marketing Officer, MyBuys; former Senior Vice President of Marketing, Intaact Corporation

Dan has definite points of view. I appreciate his perspective, even though I don't always agree with him.

Kurt Shaver—Founder, The Sales Foundry

Kurt is a fellow member of the National Speakers Association. We share ideas and look for opportunities to refer each other.

Jill Konrath—Author of *Selling to BIG Companies* and *SNAP Selling*

Jill and I share information as authors and colleagues. We met just after our first books were published.

Eric Blumthal—CEO, Count 5

Eric and I met for a beer when I was in Atlanta. (You're already friends when you've been referred.)

Barbara Giamanco—President, Social Centered Selling; Co-Author of *The New Handshake: Sales Meets Social Media*

Barb and I met at a Sales 2.0 conference. She saw my name tag and said she followed me on Twitter. When I heard her presentation, I knew we were a match!

Greg Brush—Senior Vice President of Sales, InsideView

Greg told me that referrals have 10 times the return of any prospecting strategy. That got my attention.

Nancy Nardin—President, Smart Selling Tools

Nancy is the go-to person for sales-productivity tools. She always asks the right questions.

Brian Solis—Author of *The End of Business as Usual*

I heard Brian speak at a marketing event (and you know how I love those). I liked his message and decided to pay attention to his writing.

Rich Dorfman—Partner and Vice President of Client and Professional Services, Convergent Computing

Rich contributed great insights to my presentations at the Microsoft Worldwide Partner Conference. He continues to share his perspectives about sales and technology.

Geoffrey James— Marketing Expert; *Inc.* Columnist; Author

Geoffrey interviewed me for articles in *Selling Power* magazine. We are a mutual admiration society.

Christine Crandell—President, New Business Strategies

Having a well-oiled company requires more than just aligning sales and marketing. Christine knows how to make it happen.

Ernie Almonte—Chief Visionary Officer and CEO, Almonte Group, LLC

Ernie presented at a CPA meeting for emerging professionals. That's when I heard the poignant quote you read in the book.

Tom Miller—Founder and Managing Director, Miller and Miller; former Vice President of Channel Management, Sage (U.K.) Ltd

Tom has an amazing background and a welcoming smile. I wanted his insights from a channel re-seller perspective.

Marge Bieler—CEO, RareAgent; Social Media and Content Manager, GT Software

Marge is a huge evangelist for referrals. (Love that!)

Doug Landis—Vice President of Productivity, Box

Doug has a refreshing perspective on sales and what it takes to run a successful sales team.

George Springer—Former Sales and Service Engineer, Greenleaf Corporation

George has the perspective of a "feet on the street" seasoned salesperson in a commoditized business.

Susan RoAne—The "Original" Networking Expert; Bestselling Author of *How to Work a Room*

Susan is a neighbor, colleague, and friend.

Matt Heinz—President, Heinz Marketing, Inc.; Author of *Successful Social Selling*

Matt knows marketing. Matt knows "social." His thinking is leading-edge and relevant.

The following is a list of people quoted in the book, but whom I didn't interview. I don't know most of them personally, but I found their perspectives genius and their research fascinating:

- Megan Heuer—Vice President of Data-Driven Marketing, SiriusDecisions
- John Naisbitt, Author of *Megatrends* (and several other international bestsellers)
- Reid Hoffman—Executive Chairman and Co-Founder, LinkedIn; Co-Author of *The Start-Up of You*
- Eric Schmidt—Executive Chairman, Google
- Stephen Spinelli and Rob Adams—Authors of *New Venture Creation*
- Woody Allen—American Actor and Director
- Jay Baer—Marketing Keynote Speaker and Bestselling Author
- Robin Dunbar—Evolutionary Psychologist
- Drake Bennett—*Businessweek* Writer
- Morten Hansen—Author of *Collaboration*
- Miles Austin—a.k.a., The Web Tools Guy
- Trish Bertuzzi—President, The Bridge Group
- Benny Evangelista—*San Francisco Chronicle* Writer
- Dr. David Greenfield—Assistant Clinical Professor of Psychology, University of Connecticut School of Medicine

- Jim Taylor—Psychologist
- Casey Neistat—New York-Based Filmmaker
- Sherry Turkle—Psychologist; MIT professor; Author of *Alone Together*
- Joey Reiman—Founder and CEO, BrightHouse; Author of *Thinking for a Living*
- Ken Krogue—President, InsideSales.com
- Nicholas A.C. Read and Dr. Stephen J. Bistritz—Authors of *Selling to the C-Suite*
- Stanley Milgram—Psychologist
- Henry David Thoreau—American Author

About Joanne Black

Joanne Black is America's leading authority on referral selling—the only business-development strategy proven to convert prospects into clients more than 50 percent of the time. As the founder of No More Cold Calling, Joanne helps salespeople, sales teams, and business owners build their referral networks to quickly attract more business, decrease operating costs, and ace out the competition every time.

An engaging speaker and innovative seminar leader, Joanne is changing the business of sales. In her groundbreaking book, *NO MORE COLD CALLING™: The Breakthrough System That Will Leave Your Competition in the Dust,* Joanne shows readers how to leverage the power of referrals so they get meetings at the level that counts and hit their numbers without hitting the phones. In her new book, *Pick Up the Damn Phone!*, she examines the links between technology, sales, and referrals—helping readers understand how to effectively leverage technology in sales, and when it's time to put the toys away and have a grown-up, face-to-face conversation.

Practicing what she preaches, Joanne has built her business solely through referrals. She works with clients of all sizes—from small- and medium-sized businesses to some of the biggest and most recognizable brands in the U.S.

A member of the National Speakers Association, Joanne regularly speaks at sales and incentive meetings, sales conferences, and association meetings. She holds a B.A. in English from the University of California at Berkeley and a Certificate in Training and Human Resources Development, with Honors, from the University of California Extension.

Joanne resides in the San Francisco Bay Area.

JOANNE'S BREAKTHROUGH REFERRAL-SELLING SYSTEM

No More Cold Calling is the breakthrough system that transforms your sales organization into a highly-refined, referral-generating machine. Get only qualified leads, score meetings with decision-makers, and fill your pipeline with nothing but hot leads to your ideal clients. Turn your current customers and your myriad of contacts into a rich referral network—relationships you can leverage to ace out the competition. You'll actually find qualified prospects, ready to do business, calling *you* to ask for help!

Referrals are common sense, but not common practice. Fewer than 5 percent of companies have a targeted referral system with a written referral plan, weekly referral goals, accountability, and methods to track and measure results.

Beat the Competition

No other business-development strategy generates *only* qualified leads—prospects who actually want to take your call. When you receive referral introductions, you're pre-sold and have already earned your prospects' trust. You reduce the cost of sales, shorten your sales process, make the competition simply disappear, and convert prospects into clients more than 50 percent of the time.

It really is this simple: While others are making calls, you're meeting clients. So implement a referral program, and drive your sales needle off the charts.

The Missing Link

No More Cold Calling provides the essential prospecting link missing from every organization's sales process: An actual referral system—a step-by-step process with goals, accountability, and metrics that you can implement immediately. Fast impact. Simple. Easy to quantify.

Selected Speaking Topics

The following is a sampling of Joanne's most popular presentations. She regularly introduces new topics and tailors speaking engagements to each client's needs. If you want a unique sales speaker for your next meeting, contact Joanne first. Find out how her referral-selling expertise can help your sales team.

Pick Up the Damn Phone!

It's people, not technology, that seal the deal. Discover how to leverage technology for sales—and when it's time to put away the toys and have a grown-up, face-to-face conversation.

Pack Your Pipeline with HOT Prospects

Tap into Joanne's proven No More Cold Calling® Referral-Selling System. Boost your sales and rev up your business! Hit your sales numbers without hitting the phones.

Ditch the Sales Pitch

Top salespeople don't pitch. They let their results speak for themselves by answering the toughest, most important question sales professionals will ever face: "Why should clients work with you?"

Double Your Referral Network in 90 Days

Boost your sales visibility, strengthen relationships with current clients, attract new ones, and meet top-notch referral sources.

Get the Trash Out of Your Funnel: Lead Generation That Works

Attracting the wrong kind of clients is like dumping trash into your sales funnel. Measure the effectiveness of your funnel by the quality, not quantity, of leads—and only work with your ideal clients.

9 Killer Steps to Boost Your Sales

With these vital business-development steps, you'll accelerate your win ratio and outsmart the competition.

Put the "Social" Back in Social Media

Social media isn't the next big thing in sales; you are! Get real, get in touch, and get ahead by understanding how social media expands your referral relationships.

Let's Talk!

Want to start leveraging the power of referrals for your company? To learn more about No More Cold Calling's referral-selling programs and resources, visit www.nomorecoldcalling.com. Or pick up the phone and contact Joanne at 415-461-8763 or joanne@nomorecoldcalling.com.

MORE GREAT READS FROM BOOKTROPE

Strategic Sale Presentations **by Jack Malcolm** (Business - Sales) When your big moment comes, will you be ready? Strategic Sales Presentations prepares you for the presentations that could make or break you as an accomplished sales professional.

Bottom Line Selling **by Jack Malcolm** (Business - Sales) An indispensable tool for sales professionals: how to effectively present your value proposition.

The Forecast Fatale **by Brian Schlosser** (Business Guidance in a Noir Mystery) A wisecracking business detective in the city that seldom buys, and an introduction to sales professionalism with essential advice called out.

The Art of Grant Writing **by Sharon Charnell Gherman** (Business Writing) A "must read" for anyone writing proposals. You'll learn how to streamline your proposal process, get tips to help you work more efficiently, and find examples that will make your work easier.

The Art of Selling Real Estate **by Patricia Cliff** (Real Estate) Practical advice for selling real estate in today's challenging market.

Discover more books and learn about our new approach to publishing at **booktrope.com**.

33374193R00131

Made in the USA
Charleston, SC
12 September 2014